*the*

# SMART

# *Groom's*

# ANSWER GUIDE

# Praise for
## *Complete Guide to the First Five Years of Marriage,*

from which this book is adapted:

"Keeping this book handy can help you build a relationship that stays afloat in spite of money worries, sexual storms . . . and confused communication."

> GARY SMALLEY
> Author, *The DNA of Relationships*

"What happens in the first five years of marriage will largely determine the quality of the marriage for years to come. Here is a book that gives the practical help every couple needs to build a healthy marriage. It should be required reading for all newly married couples."

> GARY D. CHAPMAN, PH.D.
> Author, *The Five Love Languages*
> and *The Four Seasons of Marriage*

"Written by an extraordinary team of counselors . . . filled with practical, biblical advice. You have questions? They have answers! Buy one book for yourself and ten more to use as wedding gifts!"

> CAROL KENT
> Speaker and author of *When I Lay My Isaac Down*

"This new Focus on the Family book is so timely and important for you to read if you're a newly married couple—or to give to that newly married couple in your life. Let this incredible team of marriage and family experts get your marriage off to a great start."

JOHN TRENT, PH.D.
President, The Center for Strong Families
and author of *Breaking the Cycle of Divorce*

"This book is a gem. . . . Packed with wisdom. A perfect gift for any newlywed or engaged couple."

GARY THOMAS
Author, *Sacred Marriage* and *Sacred Influence*

FOCUS ON THE FAMILY®

# *the* SMART
# GROOM'S
## ANSWER GUIDE

*an eye-opening look at your first year of marriage*

GENERAL EDITORS

WILFORD WOOTEN, L.M.F.T. & PHILLIP J. SWIHART, PH.D.

Tyndale House Publishers, Inc., Carol Stream, Illinois

# Contents

# The Authors

Lon Adams, M.A., L.M.F.T.

Sheryl DeWitt, L.M.F.T., L.M.F.C.C.

Daniel Huerta, M.S.W., L.C.S.W.

Romie Hurley, L.P.C., N.C.C.

Rob Jackson, M.S., L.P.C., L.M.H.C., N.C.C.

Betty Jordan, R.N., M.A., L.P.C.

Sandra Lundberg, Psy.D.

Glenn Lutjens, M.A., L.M.F.T.

Phillip J. Swihart, Ph.D.

Mitch Temple, M.S., L.M.F.T.

Wilford Wooten, M.S.W., L.M.F.T., L.C.S.W.

# ACKNOWLEDGMENTS

We appreciate the monumental editing needed for a volume encompassing the work of so many diverse authors, which was provided by John Duckworth, Senior Book Producer, Focus on the Family. We also wish to recognize our colleague Aarin Hovanec for her perceptive observations and comments. In addition, we're thankful for Sharon Manney's technical assistance in the preparation of this manuscript.

# INTRODUCTION

When it comes to the Indianapolis 500, it may be difficult to predict which lap will be most critical. But in a marriage, the first five years are central. That's when key adjustments are made and expectations are tested.

How you deal with the large and small crises of your marriage at the start sets important patterns for the future. That's true for brides *and* grooms, no matter whether you tend to run in panic or stay and bury your feelings.

Most marriages start with the delight of "being in love" and honeymoon excitement. The question is what happens next. One spouse put it this way: "I thought the first year would be wonderful. It was hell."

During the first few years, couples "get naked" in more ways than one. And physical nakedness can be much less revealing than many other kinds.

Even in marriages that end up thriving, marital stressors may be—or at least seem to be—more intense in the beginning than later. For instance, it's stressful to find that neither of you seems to have any conflict management skills. As one comedian noted, "My wife and I never fight; we just have moments of intense fellowship."

And then there's sex. Whatever happened to the glorious expectations you had in that wonder-world of dating? It may only take a few months of marital reality for the fantasies of "true love" and sexual excitement to clash with the disappointments of sharing a bed with another imperfect person who's sometimes tough to like, let alone love.

The spiritual dimension of your relationship can be a point of contention early in your marriage, too. These years often form fertile ground for spiritual attack by an enemy who would love to destroy a relationship that God has blessed as holy.

Many of the challenges of the first years stem from distorted expectations. We live in a fast-food culture with a sense of entitlement to having everything happen on demand. But marriage doesn't work that way.

The apostle Paul advised Christians to "work out your salvation with fear and trembling" (Philippians 2:12). As radio Bible teacher Alistair Begg has noted, we need to do the same in our marriages.

This is a book about working things out—trembling or otherwise. In the pages to follow you'll find answers to questions commonly asked by grooms and grooms-to-be. You'll probably find some issues you're struggling with. It's our hope and prayer that this book will be a rich source of help and encouragement on your journey through the partnership called marriage.

There's another distinctive to this volume, too. The many authors who've contributed have a working relationship with Focus on the Family. Most are professional staff members with Focus on the Family's counseling department. All are committed Christians and highly qualified, licensed mental health, marriage, and family therapists with many years of combined experience in working with thousands of couples and individuals across America.

The early years of marriage are a special adventure. As you

explore your new partnership, explore this book, too. We believe you'll find it to be a thought-provoking source of creative solutions for meeting the challenges of your first years together.

—*Wilford Wooten and Phillip J. Swihart*
*General Editors*

# What Does It Mean to Be a Husband?

*1*

*"A man is not where he lives, but where he loves."*
—LATIN PROVERB

John was working long hours at his office, providing financially for his family. That, he believed, was his duty as a husband. Seldom at home, he didn't realize what his schedule was doing to the foundation of the family he was trying to establish.

Before he knew it, he was living by himself.

Stunned, he asked himself why his wife had suddenly left him.

The warning signs had been there, but John had been too busy to recognize them. The fact was that he'd developed a skewed perspective of his role as a man and husband several years before marrying Susan. As a young man he'd watched his father work long hours, and came to believe that his identity and level of success depended on how others saw his accomplishments. Compliments drove his work ethic.

John was struggling with loving and accepting himself. He worked long and hard to gain the praise of others—but neglected his family because building a strong marriage usually doesn't earn many accolades.

What does it mean to be a husband? John thought he knew, but discovered otherwise.

You don't have to make the same mistake. Here are some qualities found in Ephesians 5:19-33 that help define what a husband is and does.

1. *Love shown in sacrifice and commitment.* A husband's love needs to be unselfish. It's not always tied to sexual desire, which by its nature is self-seeking.

How might things have been different for John if, when awakening every morning, he'd started the day by figuring out how to make it a special one for Susan? That act of sacrificial, committed, unselfish love could have revolutionized their relationship.

Love from a husband also needs to be natural, not dutiful. Making sacrifices out of mere duty isn't an expression of love; it may just be an effort to avoid failure and pain. That's not to say that loving deeds will always be accompanied by warm feelings; sometimes the actions come first and the feelings are a step behind.

2. *Leadership and courage.* Leaders need to first learn how to serve (see Matthew 20:26). Then they can lead through example. In John's case, he could have helped his family by showing how to express unconditional love, set boundaries, provide guidance, exercise self-control, and manage money.

Husbands need courage, too. But that quality isn't just about driving through thunderstorms and stopping burglars. A husband also needs the courage to admit his mistakes, and to participate in his own growing and maturing process.

3. *Sound priorities.* A husband must learn about his wife's needs, put them above his own, and respond to them—physically and emotionally. John needed to say no to his competitive drive sometimes.

He needed to learn that the most rewarding thing—above applause, recognition, money, success, and attention—is being able to love another person to the point that you would give your life for her.

That's not to say that a husband must erase his boundaries and individuality. It's important to maintain friendships, dreams, goals, vision, and "healthy space." But a "me first" attitude is the opposite of the one commanded in Scripture (see Philippians 2:3-4).

4. *Communication and thanksgiving.* A husband needs to keep learning more about his wife and to communicate verbally and non-verbally. It's not healthy to trust only in yourself.

Just as a man can't read a woman's mind, a woman can't read a man's. Take time to share your thoughts. Let your spouse into your life.

5. *Unity.* The marriage covenant represents the greatest unity a man will ever have. It's a closeness that's above that between parents and children and among friends.

Both Old and New Testaments (Genesis 2:24; Ephesians 5:31) affirm that husband and wife "will become one flesh." There's a unity that goes beyond the physical.

Joan and Bill are examples of what happens when these principles are applied in a marriage.

Recently married, Bill was getting involved in as many things as possible at work in an attempt to "move up" in his career. He was trying to establish what he called "a good name."

Joan was also working full-time, but was home in the evenings. As a result, she spent many lonely nights and weekends waiting for Bill to come home. The couple's romance and intimacy were becoming nonexistent.

Joan asked Bill to begin saying no to work requests that weren't essential. He listened to her need to connect and began to set limits on his job commitments.

This was difficult for him initially, but the relationship began to thrive. He began to feel better about himself. He noticed that things were even improving at work, too.

It was clear that God was honoring Bill's commitment to listen and respond to his wife. If only John had made that commitment while he still had the opportunity.

What does it mean to be a husband? There are many steps a man takes in his marital journey, but the first—and perhaps most important—is committing himself to fulfilling his God-ordained purpose of meeting his wife's needs.

—*Daniel Huerta*

## Taking It Personally

1. How do you think your parents—or others who raised you— would answer the "What does it mean to be a husband?" question? How might their answers have influenced your views on this subject?

2. What appeals to you most about becoming a husband? Try writing a one-page job description that starts with that "duty" and includes at least four other things you'd enjoy.

# Why Isn't My Wife the Person I Thought She Was?

*2*

Was your wife someone different before you got married? Has she changed for the worse over time?

It's much more likely that you saw her through rose-colored glasses while you were dating, and now the glasses are off. And guess what? You're probably not the person she thought *you* were, either.

Before the wedding, differences tend to seem intriguing, interesting, and attractive. A few months or years into the marriage, however, what seemed so inviting in the semi-fantasy world of dating now seems considerably less than idyllic.

That beautiful angel you married turns out to be a real woman. She has flaws that weren't previously apparent. She may handle things in ways that you find inefficient, and isn't interested in your suggestions about how to do them differently—even though, from your viewpoint, your ways are obviously superior.

You discover to your shock that she has the capacity to express a range of emotions not plumbed in your dating days. You hadn't felt that hot edge of her temper nor the cold, steely glare she now feels free to display.

Perhaps your wife has expectations you never guessed were there. You assumed hers would match yours—and they don't.

How do these "mistakes" occur?

Barbie and Carl were so in love. They wanted to be with each other constantly. Unable to endure the thought of a long, drawn-out courtship, they married within three months of their first meeting.

Barbie was a life-of-the-party sort of girl—a social butterfly. A former high school cheerleader, she was bubbly and happy-go-lucky.

Carl was an A student in college. He had serious career plans in accounting and business. He liked books and challenging discussions about theology and politics. Not having dated many girls, he was in a daze when Barbie was willing to go out with him.

Barbie saw Carl as a responsible, mature man who'd provide stability and security in her life. Carl saw Barbie as the perfect compliment to his otherwise rather pedestrian life.

They quickly decided they were perfect for each other. Surely they'd have no problems that couldn't easily be resolved.

Two years into their marriage, though, there was a deep rift in their relationship. Carl was coming home from the office just wanting to read a book or have some quiet space. He didn't want to talk to Barbie about her day or her shopping plans for the next. At bedtime he didn't feel very amorous.

Barbie seemed frustrated and angry when Carl had no interest in dinner parties or going out dancing with her old friends. Going to church on Sunday mornings was more than enough social life for him.

Carl was angry and frustrated, too. Barbie was chronically late and seemed not to care how annoying this was to him. She was running up bills on the credit card and was irresponsible about paying them. She visited the hair salon frequently, apparently wanting to look very sexy when going out. In his view she was a terrible housekeeper, leaving the place in a mess most of the time.

What had gone so terribly wrong with this relationship? Had Barbie really changed?

Carl and Barbie were opposites—and always had been. "Opposites attract" may be a common phenomenon but doesn't necessarily lead to a strong marriage. Far too often what seemed irresistible in the swirl of hormones and emotional highs during a fast courtship turns out to be irritating in the 24/7, "up close and personal" daily life of husband and wife.

The mature and responsible guy seems to become a stiff, nit-picking perfectionist, boring and sexually uninteresting. The girl who appeared to be such a wonderful, bouncy, free spirit now looks like an irresponsible, immature twit with no depth at all.

Is that what's happened with your wife? The truth is that she's the same woman you fell so much in love with. But *you* have changed—stripped of your illusions about her. You're disappointed.

So what should you do?

You might find it helpful to sit down and list the reasons why you chose this particular woman to be your wife. Think of all her attributes that you enjoy and value. Think of yourself as the author of the Song of Solomon, writing about your bride. Shift your focus from the negative and critical to the positive and appreciative.

Then make a date to share these thoughts with her.

If this seems impossible, consider the very real possibility that your marriage is at a crossroads. Disappointment may be making you vulnerable to the attentions of others, who you might imagine would better meet your needs and expectations. Or you may just be resigning yourself to years of regret about your choice of a spouse, bitter that you're obligated to stay in a marriage without any hope of realizing your dreams.

If this describes you, it's past time for you and your wife to seek marriage counseling. Find a Christian professional who won't reinforce the lie that happiness lies just around the corner if only you escape from this mistake and move on to something new.

Your situation is not at all hopeless. But it does require a fresh perspective and some tools to employ in developing a more mature relationship.

*—Phillip J. Swihart*

## Taking It Personally

1. If you're a groom-to-be, what change in your wife-to-be would bother you most? If you're already married, what change would you warn your pre-marriage self about if you could?

2. Silently or out loud, practice communicating your frustration to your wife in a way that doesn't leave her feeling disrespected. You could begin by completing this sentence: "When it seems to me that you've become more _____, I feel _____."
Then have this conversation when both of you are rested and not pressed for time.

# Why Isn't My Wife
# More Like Mom?

*3*

Kevin had it all—a good education, a successful career, and a brand new, beautiful bride named Terri. He was a smart guy. But, like many men, Kevin made a very common mistake.

It was all quite innocent. But he asked Terri one of the most potentially controversial questions any man could ask his new wife (other than, "Can we have sex again?").

"Terri," he said, "why aren't you more like Mom?"

As you can imagine, Kevin didn't have time to explain himself. As soon as the words escaped his lips, Terri broke down in tears and ran out of the room, devastated.

Through the double-bolted door and between Terri's sobs, Kevin tried to explain what he really meant to say. He hadn't intended to hurt his wife. But he couldn't vindicate himself.

Often when young husbands ask a question like that, they're attempting to make a suggestion, "just something to consider." But young wives, who are often very self-conscious in their new roles, usually don't see it that way. They view it as a comparison with the woman their husbands have idealized since birth. They see themselves placed side by side with a person who has at least 20 or 30 years of successful domestic experience under her belt. They conclude, "How can I compare to that?"

By the time sons marry, many mothers have mastered the art of preparing flawless meals and cleaning the house to spotless status in record time. Or at least their sons remember them that way. It's easy to forget that Mom made her share of domestic blunders and was once inexperienced herself. Sons tend to recall Mom as the queen of the world who could prepare an exquisite Italian dinner while simultaneously rewiring the house.

It's easy for a husband to assume that his new bride knows how to prepare common dishes—but she may not. He may think she'll clean and cook at the same level as his mother. But a young wife simply hasn't had the opportunity to master those skills—and may not have the inclination.

Many new husbands have made the "comparing wife to mother statement" or implied the same nonverbally. A wise man is one who can learn from and grow through his mistakes—or at least the mistakes of others. So, based on the experiences of fellow husbands who have said the wrong thing, here are a few principles to remember.

1. *Comparing your spouse with others illuminates her flaws.* It's like painting a mole on her face bright red; everybody will notice it.

Comparing your wife to your mother puts your spouse in a position where she'll fall short no matter what. After all, most of us tend to compare the "model" person's best assets to apparent weaknesses in the other.

Consider how unfair it would be for a wife to compare her new husband to her father. The latter might make twice the money the son-in-law did at his age, act as CEO of his own company, spend all his free time with his family, and serve as an elder in his church. No man could measure up to that kind of example. It would be like comparing Homer Simpson to Abraham.

Instead of comparing, try accepting and encouraging your wife. These biblical instructions apply to spouses, too:

"Accept one another, then, just as Christ accepted you, in order to bring praise to God" (Romans 15:7).

"Therefore encourage one another and build each other up, just as in fact you are doing" (1 Thessalonians 5:11).

2. *Learn to see your spouse through God's eyes.* God created David with distinctive strengths, yet David had obvious failings. In some ways he wouldn't have compared favorably with many ancient Israelites. Though a great king, he was a failure as a father. Though strong in battle, he was a poor warrior against lust. Yet, with all his flaws, God said David was a man after His own heart.

We can be glad that God doesn't judge or place value on us by comparing our weakness to other's strengths. You can follow His example by valuing your wife as the unique individual God created her to be—not as a faint echo of your mom.

3. *List and thank God for your wife's good qualities.* Sit down and compile a list of positive characteristics you see in your wife. If you've let yourself become nearsighted when it comes to seeing her good qualities, ask a mature Christian who knows both of you well to help you in this process.

After you identify these qualities, talk to God about them. Thank Him for each attribute. Ask Him to help you recognize and value this quality daily. If you do this consistently, you'll tend to compare less.

4. *Sing your wife's praises.* A "wife of noble character" is described in Proverbs 31. The author, King Lemuel, must have known the value of recognizing and extolling a spouse's good attributes. He saw and praised this bride as trustworthy, conscientious, and industrious. He touted her as a woman who managed her money well and who deserved the highest level of honor from her children and her husband. Note his final observation in verse 29: "Many women do noble things, but you surpass them all."

What a wise and compassionate man! If you insist on comparing your spouse to others, remember King Lemuel's example—and make sure you compare your wife in a positive way.

Focusing on your mate's strengths and beauty has a way of diminishing the tendency to spotlight her weaknesses. Isn't that what true love is all about?

*—Mitch Temple*

## TAKING IT PERSONALLY

1. If your relationship with your mom were documented in home videos, what would be the highlights?

2. If your mother is still living, think of one thing she hasn't quite mastered that your wife (or wife-to-be) is good at. For example, your bride may be able to upgrade an e-mail program for your mom, who can't tell a firewall from a fireplace. Next time you're all together, brag a little about your bride's skill (without putting your mom down) and offer her services if she's willing.

# Why Does She Want to Talk All the Time?

4

Bill is avoiding his wife, Carol.

He knows he's doing it, too. And he feels guilty about it.

But he thinks it's the only way to deal with his predicament.

He can't seem to handle her frequent demands for conversation. He feels that she nags him continually. When he just wants to relax, she has another emotional outburst about how he never talks to her.

Bill hasn't told Carol exactly how he feels about all this. He doesn't want her to get angry or hurt.

But Carol is already both of those things. She can't believe Bill chose once again to spend Saturday golfing with his buddies. She was looking forward to spending the day with him, hoping they could find some of the closeness they once shared.

She feels rejected. The more he avoids talking with her, the more insecure she feels and the harder she tries to get him to "open up."

If you're feeling nagged to talk, you're probably feeling overwhelmed, too. Avoidance may seem like the only solution for relief. This relief is only temporary, though, because it leaves your spouse without resolution—and often determined to try harder.

You may begin to feel like a trapped victim, at the mercy of your spouse's "need to talk." Worse yet, you may anticipate another session of having your shortcomings pointed out.

Avoidance doesn't work. But here are some suggestions if you're feeling cornered by a spouse who always seems to be asking, "Can we talk?"

1. Take the initiative to spend time doing things together *other* than talking.

2. Go to a Christian bookstore and buy a book about communication in marriage. Read from it aloud to your spouse and ask her questions about her reactions.

3. Share a chore, like doing the dishes. You may find yourself communicating during the dull moments.

4. When she's not expecting it, ask her what she really needs. Say, "How can I show you I love you?" or, "What would make your day easier?"

5. Put the newspaper away, neglect a hobby, or shut the TV off in order to spend time with your spouse.

6. Keep a sense of humor. Find cartoons about how different men and women are, and how they communicate. Make more fun of your own gender than the other person's.

These are all good things to do, but it's also important for you to ask for the peace and quiet you may need. Otherwise, you'll probably feel like a helpless victim of your mate's demands.

One way to do this is to set a specific time to talk. This should thrill your spouse, since it represents a commitment to communicate. The limits need to be spelled out, though, in order to avoid false expectations. Your spouse may be thinking of a marathon conversation, while you may dread anything longer than a TV sitcom.

Try 20 or 30 minutes to start. That's probably the most you'd want for a serious discussion. Pray at the beginning and the end if you like. Get a kitchen timer and stick to the limit. Promise not to run, but allow for a time-out if things get too intense.

What should you do during that time? Here are some ideas.

- Explore and discuss your needs for communication.
- Explore and discuss your needs for quiet or alone time.
- Explore and discuss your needs for outside friendships and recreation.
- Use "I" statements to convey feelings of being pressured, over-whelmed, or discouraged. This will help keep your spouse from feeling attacked. For example: "I feel hopeless when I hear 'We need to talk,' because it reminds me of my mom. She always used that phrase when I was in trouble." This is better than, "You're just like my mom!" The goal is for the speaker to feel heard and understood.
- If you need to take a time-out, be sure to schedule a reunion within 24 hours for further discussion. This gives both of you a sense of reassurance and safety.

If Bill and Carol follow these suggestions, here's what probably will happen.

Bill will feel more in control, seeing how to give Carol what she needs without fearing it will never be enough. He'll grow more assertive in asking for what he needs, and less guilty about taking time for himself.

Carol will feel less threatened, emotional, and needy. She'll be happier, more content. She'll know Bill loves her because he's been initiating doing things together—and even asking about her feelings.

—*Romie Hurley*

## Taking It Personally

1. When your wife (or wife-to-be) wants to talk, especially about your relationship, do you tend to feel nagged, threatened, guilty, bored, curious, or glad? Why?

2. Set a specific time to talk this week—20 or 30 minutes to start. Let your mate choose the topic. If the conversation flags, try asking questions about her needs and feelings. Come prepared to reveal at least one emotion you've felt recently; if you aren't sure how to talk about feelings, try jotting down some thoughts beforehand to get you started.

# How Can We Communicate Without Talking?

*5*

When Paige and her husband, Steve, sit down to talk, she's usually intimidated. She knows Steve loves her, but he hardly ever smiles. *Is he mad at me?* she wonders.

Chuck isn't much of a conversationalist. He knows that's frustrating to his wife, Raina, who could talk the paint off the side of a barn. He wishes there were a way to let her know he cares—without having to chat for hours at a time.

Cherie doesn't understand why her husband Brian got so upset yesterday when she left him a Post-It note on the kitchen table. All it said was, "Remember, garbage day." She was just reminding him to take out the trash. Would he have been happier if she'd drawn a little smiley face on it?

Unspoken communication—a raised eyebrow, a folding of the arms across the chest, a hand on the shoulder, an e-mail—can be at least as powerful as words. It can help build your marriage—or chip away at it.

Communicating without talking can be tricky. You may not always realize what you're "saying." And your silent messages may contradict your spoken ones, confusing your spouse.

It's no wonder some wives begin to ask early in their marriages, "Why does my husband say one thing and act totally different?" Some husbands, on the other hand, ask, "If she's really attracted to me as she used to be, why does she act like a cold potato every time I approach her?"

The unspoken can be very difficult to interpret properly. Nevertheless, nonverbal communication has its positive side. To help you and your mate make the most of those silent messages, here are some principles to remember:

1. *Go low-tech when possible.* When it comes to communicating with your spouse, don't try to send important messages or work out sensitive issues over the phone or via e-mail.

When you read an e-mail or listen on the phone, you're not getting the whole message. You can't interpret facial expressions, maintain eye contact, or sense warmth or genuineness. If intimate, relationship-building conversation is needed, have it face-to-face.

2. *Don't be "all talk."* Remember this advice: "Faith by itself, if it is not accompanied by action, is dead" (James 2:17). Actions do speak louder than words. You can tell a hungry man you care about him and wish him well, but if you don't demonstrate your compassion the words are useless. The same is true for your spouse.

A church sign put it this way: "Actions speak louder than bumper stickers." Ask yourself whether the messages you've been sending your spouse lately have been through your actions—or the lack thereof.

3. *Don't rely on silence to send a message.* Silence can be one of the loudest forms of communication, but it's easily misinterpreted. What does it tend to say in your marriage? Is it "I don't want to fight"? "I'd

rather not say anything that could stir up trouble"? "Don't bother me"? "I don't care what you think or what you need from me"?

The trouble with silence is that your mate may "fill in the blanks" with answers that aren't correct. Learning to communicate what you feel will help your spouse know what's in your heart—instead of encouraging her to take your silence and assume the worst.

4. *Don't catastrophize.* In other words, don't overreact. What you *think* your spouse meant may not be what she intended to communicate.

Ask for clarification: "Remember the other day when I asked you about taking a vacation and you sighed real loud? Were you aggravated with me because I brought it up again, or were you frustrated with yourself for having forgotten about it?"

5. *Watch your body language.* Your facial expressions and eye contact send messages to your spouse about how interested you are in what she is saying.

Actions like looking away, cleaning your fingernails, yawning, or flipping channels on the remote say, "I have better things to do." To avoid getting distracted when your spouse is trying to communicate with you, turn off the radio, TV, computer, or other electronic devices.

6. *Use touch to communicate your love.* When Jesus wanted to communicate how valuable children were to His kingdom, He didn't just say, "Hey, kids, you are valuable!" He reached down and touched them and sat them in His lap.

People need touch. Babies left untouched become ill emotionally and physically. Spouses who fail to affectionately touch each other by holding hands, rubbing necks, putting their arms around each other, and hugging will not be as close—literally and figuratively—as those who make these patterns part of their everyday routine.

7. *Use your eyes to express warmth and caring.* Most mothers are experts at controlling their children's behavior by simply looking at them; sometimes it seems a mom's angry look in church can pierce 70 rows of bodies to reprimand a talking teenager. In marriage, your eyes can communicate warmth or disgust, contentment or dissatisfaction, love or hatred, approval or disappointment.

Many men struggle with looking at their wives. Some are by nature shy and developed a habit in childhood to avoid looking directly at a speaker. Some fear seeing disappointment in their wives' eyes. Whatever the case, both men and women need to look their spouses in the eyes, especially when discussing sensitive topics or expressing love.

8. *Practice, practice, practice.* Make sure that what you feel in your heart is communicated clearly not just by your words, but also by eye contact, touch, and other "nonverbals." Don't assume that since you feel good about what you're communicating, your spouse must feel good about it, too.

—*Mitch Temple*

## TAKING IT PERSONALLY

1. If you and your bride (or bride-to-be) took a vow of silence for 90 days, how might it affect your relationship? What would you miss most?

2. Next time you and your mate have a conversation, pay attention to what you may be communicating nonverbally. Avoid glancing at your watch, looking past or "through" her, or frowning when you're just thinking or listening carefully. Lean forward slightly, make eye contact, and nod to indicate you've heard what she's said. Afterward, consider: Did the conversation last longer than usual? Did your partner seem more satisfied with the talk? Did your actions seem to influence hers? What can you learn from this experience that might be applied to future conversations?

# What Does It Mean to Be the Spiritual Leader?

*6*

Kim and Trevor were highly involved at their church. They enjoyed serving in various roles, while trying to make sure they didn't spend so much time on church work that they couldn't nurture their new marriage.

When Kim was asked to take charge of a preschool choir, she hesitated. She'd need time to pray and discuss the opportunity with Trevor, she said. After all, her husband was the spiritual leader of their home.

When you hear that story, how do you react? Is Kim right in thinking of her husband as the spiritual leader? Or does she sound like a throwback to the days of pilgrim hats and porridge?

Many people these days would pick the latter. At the very least, they'd have questions about the idea of husbands exercising spiritual leadership.

Some husbands wonder, "What am I supposed to do, act like a preacher?"

Some wives ask, "Why is *he* supposed to be the only spiritual leader? Why can't we both do it?"

Others say, "My husband's not interested in leading. What am I supposed to do?"

These questions have at least two things in common. First is an acknowledgment that families need leaders. Second is the issue of control: Who's really in charge, and why?

While the Bible clearly affirms the equality of men and women (see Galatians 3:28), God assigned the responsibility of spiritual leadership to husbands: "Wives, submit to your husbands, as is fitting in the Lord. Husbands, love your wives and do not be harsh with them" (Colossians 3:18-19).

Differing roles don't mean, however, that God considers wives inadequate, less important, or less responsible as "suitable helpers" (see Genesis 2:18). Only an unwise man would reject his wife's opinions and assistance, since God created her to be his best earthly resource.

Where does this leave the Christian woman whose husband is an unbeliever—or uninterested in spiritual leadership? Like the single Christian woman, she still has a Husband who nurtures and equips her. Like all Christian women (and men), she answers first to God.

The wife whose husband can't or won't be the spiritual leader is to be an example to him and a representative of Christ. She resists participating in anything—pornography, for example—that would bring him spiritual harm. If he causes physical, mental, or spiritual hurt to her or their children, she carries out her duty to leave with them immediately, lest she endanger him by enabling him to sin.

But what about husbands and wives who share an active faith in Christ? What is a spiritual leader supposed to *do*?

Christians have varying opinions on the mechanics of this question. In fact, this may be one of the most divisive issues in the church today.

Generally speaking, if a Christian husband and wife have a healthy relationship, they make decisions together as equals—

agreeing that Christ is the ultimate Head of their home. They compare their individual aptitudes and assume tasks based on their strengths. In some areas of service they share tasks. But they both recognize that the husband carries the greater responsibility for leadership.

A spiritual servant-leader is ready to protect, help, and defend. For instance, if his wife is being treated badly by a parent, in-law, or boss, a man following Christ's example will sacrifice relational comfort when necessary to come to her defense.

A true spiritual leader imitates Christ. He's attuned to his family's needs, providing physical support, grace, and encouragement. He's concerned for the spiritual welfare of family members and takes initiative to help them grow in their relationship with God.

Even in hard times, he doesn't regard this role as boring or overly difficult. It's what he was made for. Not just willing to die for the members of his family, he's ready to live for them, too.

Since spiritual leadership grows from a man's relationship with Christ, it defies a simple description. But here are a few ideas to help you get a better picture of the qualities needed.

1. *Connection to God.* He seeks his happiness in Christ first, realizing he can lead effectively only if he has an intimate relationship with God. Understanding he has nothing to give if he doesn't first receive from God, he looks for spiritual sustenance so he'll be able to feed his family's heart.

2. *Balance.* He pursues this for the good of his faith and family. He has the freedom to enjoy his own interests, knowing it's okay to spend an occasional Saturday morning on the golf course as long as it doesn't usurp important family time. He discusses things with his wife rather than handing down unilateral decisions, finding safety in the give-and-take of their partnership.

3. *Nurture.* He attends to his family's physical health and sustenance, and considers the mental and emotional needs of each person. He seeks to superintend his family's spiritual development individually and corporately. He knows his goal is a whole, functional family, not just a bunch of polished individuals.

4. *Action.* As problems emerge, he looks for proven resources that will help. He's proactive, spotting potential challenges and solutions. Instead of waiting until things get worse, he remains on the offense, delighting in applying solutions to his loved ones' needs.

5. *Integrity.* He seeks to be the safest, most respected man known by his family. He deals with each person carefully, but with resolve, recognizing that he's a steward of what God has given him. His servant leadership inspires other family members to go beyond their duties and be imitators of Christ—and of him.

That's the kind of person Trevor was trying to be when Kim came to him about the request to oversee the children's choir. He could tell Kim was torn between her desire to please the music committee director and her concern about the added responsibility.

"What do *you* want to do?" he asked.

"I . . . really don't want to let them down," she said anxiously. "All the parents said I'd be just right for this job."

He smiled, shaking his head. This was so typical of her—wanting to please, but regretting it later. He knew the ending wouldn't be happy if she took the job out of a sense of duty.

"I'll respect whatever you decide, Kim," he said. "But I can't say it sounds like a wise investment. Sunday afternoons are always a nice time for us to be together before another busy week. I'd miss that. And I'd be concerned you might be more stressed going into your week, too."

She frowned. "I hadn't thought of it that way," she said. "You're right. I almost gave away our favorite time of the week! Do you think it would be selfish of me to turn them down?"

"Not at all," Trevor assured her. "I just appreciate your willingness to consider my advice."

"What would I do without your level head?" she said with a laugh.

"For one thing," he teased, "you'd be a lot busier."

Spiritual leadership shouldn't be a grim prospect. It should enhance a couple's relationship, and flow from each spouse's growing relationship with God.

*—Rob Jackson*

## TAKING IT PERSONALLY

1. Do you consider yourself the spiritual leader in your marriage? Why or why not?

2. As a couple, using this chapter as a starting point, write a job description for spiritual leadership in your home. Add and subtract duties and qualifications as you see fit. Then ask your mate: "What changes do you think I need to make in order to qualify for this 'position'? Are there any tasks here that you think I should delegate? What results would you like to see in a year?"

# What Does She Want from Our Love Life?

"Do you want to talk about it?" Evan's voice was flat, his eyes unable to meet Anna's.

"Yeah, I guess," she said, and shrugged.

*Looks like she's given up,* he thought.

Last night had been hard for both of them. After two and a half years of marriage, they seemed to have reached a dead end, sexually speaking. They'd tried new things, but it was a hit-or-miss process. Even when he tried to pleasure her the way she suggested, he never seemed to get it right. They both just ended up frustrated.

*What do women want?* he thought. *I mean, what does* she *want?*

Understanding what your wife wants starts with recognizing that your sexual appetites and responses aren't quite like hers. Some differences are obvious; others are more subtle. Here are some examples:

- The male body can be ready for intercourse more quickly than the female.
- A man's physical response is often "hot linked" with visual stimulation; a woman's sexual response usually takes more time and is tied to emotion.
- Some women can achieve another orgasm soon after the first, while the man's "turnaround" time is much longer.

Gender differences make things complicated enough. Beyond that, each individual's sexual response is unique.

What does your wife want from her sexual relationship with you? Here are four things most women need from their husbands.

1. *Romance.* A woman's need for emotional intimacy to precede physical intimacy is at the heart of what we call romance. But being romantic involves more than buying her roses—though they're usually a good idea. Almost any action or setting can be romantic when it holds special meaning for the participants.

Romance can mean something different to each individual, but the common factor for most women involves a feeling of being valued. Become a student of your wife at the physical, emotional, mental, and spiritual levels. Ask her what turns her on sexually. Find out what makes her feel cherished. Strive to be the world's greatest expert on her. While you learn the mechanics of pleasing her, you'll be showing her you think she's worth studying.

2. *Non-sexual touch.* A husband can easily make the mistake of thinking that "doing unto others" (see Matthew 7:12) includes approaching his wife sexually in the way he'd like her to approach him. But the application of Jesus' teaching here is to woo her as *she* desires and needs to be approached.

Men often like overtly sexual advances, but most women say they prefer a more relational approach. Your non-sexual touch throughout the day tells your wife you value her as being much more than just an object of desire. If the only time you touch her is when you want sex, the inadvertent message you send is that you want to use her body rather than love her whole person.

3. *Intimacy.* For most wives, emotional intimacy must precede physical intimacy. Respect, safety, and friendship are essential to

unlocking her heart. If you habitually criticize or make barbed jokes about her, you'll find she's not responsive sexually when she feels unsafe emotionally.

If both of you are Christians, intimacy—the connection of minds and hearts—can be a natural extension of your shared faith. It may seem strange to think in terms of being brother and sister in Christ, but it's actually the key to your deepest bond. Sharing your thoughts, goals, needs, and hurts is a way of renewing your minds together in Christ (see Romans 12:2).

4. *Purity.* A wife's sense of emotional safety depends on how much she can trust you. This isn't limited to sexual fidelity. She needs to see you being voluntarily accountable for your time, your money, your eyes, and every other aspect of your life. In other words, show her she can entrust herself to you.

A second part of her need for your purity is your role in her spiritual nurture. Servant leadership in the home carries out God's intended role for the husband to be a picture of Christ. Just as Christ laid down His life for His bride, the church, take every opportunity to pour out your life for her sake (see Ephesians 5:25-31). When your wife sees you growing, serving, and leading spiritually, it frees her to give herself to you in every way, including sexually.

Those four principles apply to most wives. But what about yours?

When you get right down to it, there's only one way to find out what your wife really wants. Ask her.

That means honest conversation, even if it's a little uncomfortable at first. Here are Evan and Anna again, trying to get that conversation going.

Evan sets two cups of coffee on the kitchen table and sits across from his wife. She's the first to speak, and the frustration tumbles out.

"I just felt so awkward last night. I always imagined sex would be easy, like a romantic movie. You know, where the characters just fall into each others' arms and automatically know what to do without any words."

Evan nods, relieved that they're finally getting things into the open. "Me, too. Those movies leave you thinking there isn't anything confusing or messy." He pauses, watching the coffee steam in his cup. "Look . . . I think we just need to say what we're thinking and wanting. If something doesn't work, we can figure it out together."

Anna shrugs again, but this time with a smile. "I guess. We're a good team on everything else. Why not this, too?"

*—Rob Jackson*

## Taking It Personally

1. Where have you tended to collect information about the role sex plays in a woman's life? From Hollywood? Past relationships? Other guys? Do these assumptions make you feel more confident about the sexual aspect of your marriage, or less? Why?

2. Read *The Way to Love Your Wife* by Clifford and Joyce Penner (Tyndale/Focus on the Family, 2007). This book, designed to help men meet their wives' sexual needs, will give you new insights into the way your spouse is "wired."

# WHY DOES MY SPOUSE SPEND SO MUCH?

*8*

Making no effort to be quiet, Graham comes to bed. It's about 1:00 A.M. Anna has been asleep for three hours, but she's wide awake now.

"Anna," says Graham, "we're never going to make it if you keep spending so much money."

Stress squeezes Anna's stomach. She knows Graham has been working on their finances. She'd like to pretend she didn't hear him, but figures she can't.

She turns toward him. "Honey, what can I do? I try not to spend too much. There are things that we need."

Graham sighs. "We *need* $50 worth of makeup from Dillard's? We *need* $120 worth of groceries a week? We *need* to buy new furniture for the living room and put up new curtains? These are *not* needs, Hon."

Anna stares at the ceiling. "Okay, the furniture and the curtains may not be needs, but my makeup and—"

Graham interrupts, "Honey, you're beautiful. You don't need to spend that kind of money on makeup."

"But that's what it costs. And I don't buy it that often." She tries to snuggle next to Graham, but he pulls away.

"Are you kidding?" he says. "I'm so stressed out, and you think you can just cuddle up and be cute and it'll all be okay. You've got to take some responsibility here, Anna. Things are not okay."

As Graham and Anna have found, it can be a huge problem between husband and wife when one of them spends–or seems to spend—too much. But it's a problem the two of you can face and conquer together, especially if you keep the following principles in mind.

1. *Understand that you're on the same team when it comes to finances.* Chances are that neither of you wants to be told by your spouse exactly how much you can spend or where you can spend it. This doesn't communicate respect or trust for one another.

You can start by agreeing that you both want the same things concerning money—a certain amount of security and a certain amount of freedom. Those amounts may not be the same, but the general goals are. More importantly, you both want to emphasize the health of your relationship over the details of accounting.

When you're on the same team, it's easier to come up with creative solutions to spending disagreements. For instance, Graham and Anna might decide that each spouse will have a certain number of dollars set aside for grooming supplies each month or each quarter—rather than spending "as needed" on a "need" that hasn't been agreed upon.

2. *Understand the underlying reasons why your spouse overspends.* Let's say a husband and wife go to the mall. The wife buys face powder and the man buys a computer program. Neither accuses the other of overspending.

But what if these people feel compelled to go back to the mall the next day or week? What if the wife buys the newest trend in eye makeup and lipstick? What if the man buys another piece of software he doesn't really require and a memory expansion card that allows him to use it? They may be trying to meet needs that purchases can't satisfy.

You've probably heard a variety of reasons for overspending: deprived childhood, privileged childhood, depression, anxiety, the thrill of the hunt. All of these have one thing in common: a search for security. Consciously or not, the spender thinks something like, "If I have this, I'll be in style." Or, "I'll be accepted." Or, "I'll be safe." Or, "I'll be okay."

Buying things doesn't provide real security. It does nothing to change God's love for us. Due to the consumerism so prevalent in our culture, it's an ongoing battle for many people to let go of the fleeting gratification of things for the long-term security of a relationship with God through Christ.

Before making a purchase, husbands and wives need to ask themselves, "What am I trying to do?" If the answer has anything to do with finding fulfillment or escaping stress or pain, don't buy the item. It will never meet that need. Instead, take your quest for security to your heavenly Father and find it in Him.

If your spouse struggles in this area, support her in seeking security from God instead of goods. A pastor or counselor can help.

3. *Understand what things cost and how often they must be purchased.* People often enter marriage with very different experiences of spending, saving, and tithing—and preconceived ideas about what things should cost.

Take that husband and wife at the mall, for example. He buys a piece of computer software; she buys makeup from a department store. Each experiences "sticker shock" over the other's purchase.

"How can you spend that much for a little eyebrow pencil?" the husband protests. "You can get a whole box of Magic Markers for the same price!"

"Look who's talking," says the wife. "You just spent more on that computer tax program than it cost to hire that guy to do our taxes last year."

Both partners end up on the defensive.

Marriage counselors sometimes have couples go through lists of purchases, mark down what they think the prices of those items would be, and compare notes. Something like this may be worthwhile if the two of you struggle with the costs of each other's purchases. You may also want to divide the same list into wants and needs, indicate how often you think each item should be purchased, and compare results.

Knowing a certain computer program is purchased once, with upgrades bought every year, for example, will help spouses agree on the real cost. So will learning that $20 worth of powder could last three months for some women and six months for others.

4. *Understand that you must live on less than you earn.* Living from one paycheck to the next isn't comfortable for anyone. It can lead each of you to feel taken for granted, used, and insecure about the future of your marriage and finances. That insecurity is heightened when you ask the question, "What if I lost my job?"

The real problem may not be your spouse's spending or earning, but a failure to budget. That was true of Graham and Anna.

Let's look in on them three months later.

They've been working on their finances, reviewing their spending and goals once a week. They've disciplined themselves to take from one area to cover another so that they don't bust their new budget.

Over a cup of coffee Graham says, "Okay, Anna. I've finished looking at our finances for this month."

"I think we did better," Anna says. "I spent more on groceries than we planned, though. Like detergent and fabric softener and stuff."

"So," Graham replies, "that explains the $150 bill at Sam's instead of the usual $100."

"Yeah," Anna says.

"How long do fabric softener and detergent usually last us?"

"At least six months."

"So it's not something we have to buy every 30 days," says Graham.

Anna shakes her head. "No, no."

Graham sighs, relieved.

—*Sandra Lundberg*

## Taking It Personally

1. How would your bride (or bride-to-be) explain her spending habits? If you had to defend those habits in court, how would you do it? If she overspends due to insecurity, how might you help her to feel more secure?

2. As a couple, read and discuss the chapter "Do We Have to Have a Budget?" in this book. Would determining in advance how much each of you can spend provide an objective way to know when one of you is overspending? Are you willing to try it for three months to find out?

# Is It Okay Not to Have Kids?

*9*

"A growing trend among young couples is to rethink the whole parenting thing," says Steve Watters, director of family formation at Focus on the Family. "Unlike their parents, who often moved into the parenting season with little hesitation, couples now often ask, 'What if we don't want to have kids?'

"As Christians, it's important to consider our motivations. What is behind those kinds of sentiments? While some couples are excited and motivated to have kids, others don't feel a natural tug—and when friends and relatives ask them about kids, they're not quite sure what to say. They can see many natural benefits of *not* having children—cost savings, ability to pursue interesting work options, ability to travel, etc. Other parents may be frightened by the pain and hardship of childbirth, or feel like they just can't fit children into their current financial situation."

Are you considering deliberately not having children? Maybe you're asking yourself questions like these:

"Is it selfish not to have children?"

"What if we think we don't have the money or the energy?"

One Christian therapist notes that in more than 25 years of marriage and family counseling, he's never had to convince anyone to have children. Still, in recent generations Western thinking has shifted, accepting an attitude of ambivalence toward children or an outright dismissal of parenthood. Couples are not only marrying later in life, thus abbreviating the childbearing years; they're choosing not to factor children into their relationship at all.

Some two-career households have elected to wait on having children—or skip it altogether—so that full attention can be given to their jobs.

Carson and June, for example, made it clear that they would get their socio-economic status settled before having kids. June was a sales rep; Carson was starting his own software design company. Neither felt any particular emotional tug about starting a family.

Their travel-filled lives didn't seem to leave any room for talking about having kids. The more successful they became, the less time they seemed to have.

On a tenth anniversary trip to South America, they finally discussed whether they would ever try to start a family. Both agreed that finding sitters for their house and dog was hard enough. Maybe they'd have time for kids someday—but not now.

Are Carson and June choosing wisely?

Biblically speaking, we can't ignore the fact that God considers parenthood an incredible blessing. As Psalm 127:3 says, "Sons are a heritage from the Lord, children a reward from him." Even more striking is the silence of Scripture with regard to a chosen state of childlessness. It doesn't appear that the Bible ever envisioned married couples who denied themselves children. On the contrary, Genesis 1:28 declares, "Be fruitful and increase in number; fill the earth and subdue it."

The current tendency to ignore or dilute that command demonstrates a rejection of God's design for humanity. From the beginning of time, in most cases adulthood meant marriage and marriage meant children; in most circumstances, today's couples should carry on that pattern and look toward a future that includes children.

Certainly there are medical conditions that prevent childbearing. Encouraging couples to have children is not meant to imply that those who suffer the pain of infertility are less obedient to God or less valued by Him.

There are also conditions that pose genetic risks. Those with a family history of a hereditary illness might choose not to bear children, perhaps deciding on adoption instead. Julie, for instance, is being treated for bipolar disorder. She believes it's hereditary. She and her husband, Stan, are praying about the wisdom of producing their own kids, versus the possibility of adoption.

If you struggle with this issue, make sure you have all the information you need. Get genetic counseling from a specialist who can tell you what the risks really are.

For most couples, however, medical concerns don't play a major role. Preserving a lifestyle or standard of living is more likely to be an issue.

Some couples, for instance, are convinced that kids are just too expensive. If that's your objection, ask yourself questions like these: "How do other people afford children? Do I need to trust God to provide for our family? Am I simply refusing to alter my own financial goals? If we really can't afford children now, might that change?"

If you're just guessing that children are beyond your budget, get the facts. A good financial planner could tell you how much it costs to raise kids, and may be able to help you come up with a plan to raise the money as well.

Other couples want to avoid the messiness of infants and toddlers. As one woman wrote, "I have a Christian friend who's married and absolutely loathes small children. The thought of changing a diaper is disgusting to her. She will probably never have children even though she's found the man she wants to spend the rest of her life with."[1]

No doubt about it: Parenting is inconvenient. Hesitations about starting a family are understandable. The responsibilities of parenthood can't be taken lightly, and there's no denying that children will bring major changes to your marriage and your individual lives. But the difficulties associated with rearing children aren't reason enough to choose childlessness.

Children bring a new dimension of joy and fulfillment to a marriage that can't be found elsewhere. Parenthood ushers in a spiritual transformation that we might otherwise forego; it forces us to look outside ourselves and act sacrificially for the benefit of another.

Self-sacrifice isn't the only fear that makes couples wary of having kids, of course. Some husbands and wives, knowing their flaws or those of their own parents, are afraid they'll make a mistake that could misshape their children's lives.

Carson's growing-up years had left him and his sister emotionally scarred. His parents had divorced when he was 12. Fearing that could happen to him and June, he didn't want to hurt children the way he'd been hurt. Besides, with his temper, what kind of dad would he make?

No parent is perfect, and children can learn from our weaknesses as well as our strengths. If you have abusive tendencies or a family history you're afraid you'll repeat, let a counselor help you. But if you're waiting to "get your act together" 100 percent, you'll wait forever.

There are many factors involved in family planning, but the most important aspect of parenthood may be this: God gives wisdom and guidance to those who seek His help, and most parents agree that with the Lord to support them the joys of parenthood far outweigh the trials.

God is the One who ultimately gives children. Be sure to consult Him in prayer; may His blessings rest on you as you look to Him for direction.

*—Lon Adams*

## TAKING IT PERSONALLY

1. Do you feel less urgency about having children than your bride (or bride-to-be) does? If so, is your reluctance mostly about preparedness, finances, freedom, or something else?

2. If readiness is an issue, what four books could you and your mate read in order to feel better prepared for parenthood? What couple could you spend time with, observing the everyday realities of parenting? How much money could you set aside in a year to cushion the shock of starting a family? Which of these steps would help you most?

# How Well Do I Need to Know My Wife?

*10*

When it comes to creating closeness in marriage, honesty is essential. But should you and your spouse know everything about each other?

What if you don't like what your spouse has to say about her past? And if there are secrets between you, will that lead to mistrust, doubt—even divorce?

When the two of you are vulnerable and transparent, it helps each of you understand where the other is coming from—which cultivates patience and compassion. But sometimes "letting it all hang out" can hurt a relationship. Where should you draw the line?

To help you know what kinds of information are really necessary, here are nine questions you *do* need to ask your spouse.

1. *"How were you raised?"*

There's no greater influence on your spouse than the way she grew up. Ask: "How did you get along with your mother and father? Were your growing-up years pleasant? Hurtful? What did you like about the way you were raised? What didn't you like? How do you think childhood may have shaped your views of the opposite sex, yourself, and intimacy (emotional and physical)? Have you dealt with any pain from the past? If so, how? If not, are you planning to do so?"

One wife discovered how valuable this kind of conversation can be. "Understanding that Brett and his mother didn't get along gave me some insight into our relationship," she said. "Brett's mother always criticized him and made him feel worthless. If he didn't please her, she would withdraw for days to punish him. Learning how his mom approached him and prefacing my confrontation by telling him I love him and I am not going anywhere but that I just want to resolve our issue, has helped a lot. Before I understood his fear of me abandoning him like his mom did, whenever I confronted him he would internalize everything so as not to upset me for fear I would leave. This never accomplished anything. Now he's willing to speak his mind with me."

Understanding your spouse in this way helps you not to take it personally when old patterns cause problems. It also helps you work together to overcome them.

2. *"How would you describe your relationship with God?"*

For Christians, marriage is a total commitment of two people to the Lord and to each other. It's a partnership intended to allow spouses to be themselves fully, to help refine each other, and to encourage each other to become the people God created them to be. For this union to be as successful as the Lord designed it to be, you need to understand how much you and your partner have in common when it comes to faith.

3. *"How do you deal with finances?"*

Tammy complained to her sister, "Larry grew up in a family where his mother took care of all the finances. She paid the bills and decided how the money was to be spent. I'm not good with finances and don't want that responsibility. I assumed that the man was responsible for the budget in the household."

Larry and Tammy needed to discuss how money was to be handled in their house. Both had come into marriage with different expectations but hadn't talked about them.

When they finally sat down and discussed finances, they decided Larry would be in charge of paying the bills because he seemed to have been gifted with financial wisdom. They mapped out a budget, and pledged that before any big purchases were made, they'd agree on them together.

4. *"How do you see the roles of husband and wife?"*

"My mom was a stay-at-home mother," Quinn said. "She took care of the house and the kids. When Kathy went back to work, we would fight all the time because she didn't take care of the house like she should."

Kathy saw things differently: "Our finances were tight, so I wanted to go back to work. But he still expects that I cook, clean, and do all the caretaking of the house. He believes that's the woman's job. I think we should share the chores because we're both working. His view of our roles is much more traditional than how I feel is best for the both of us."

It's important to find out how your spouse thinks husband-wife roles should play out in your household, and how those roles might change during the seasons of your marriage. In the case of Quinn and Kathy, they decided that while she worked they would share chores—but when she was able to stay home, Quinn would be the breadwinner and Kathy would be in charge of household upkeep.

5. *"What roles should in-laws have?"*

What part does your spouse see both sets of parents playing in your life together?

"Susan always seeks her dad's advice before she seeks mine," Caleb says. "I love her dad, but feel it's my role as her husband to have her talk things over with me first." Having been pretty independent from an early age, Caleb feels betrayed and not trusted by Susan when she involves her parents in every decision.

Melina, on the other hand, grew up without a mom. She's come to love her husband, Spencer's, mother as if she were her own, and consults her mother-in-law on many decisions. Because Spencer is so close to his folks and trusts them implicitly, he enjoys the fact that Melina is willing to seek their counsel.

The way you deal with in-laws will depend on the depth and type of relationship you have with them. Make sure you understand your spouse's view of that relationship and what that means practically.

6. *"What do you expect regarding our sexual relationship?"*

Does your spouse believe sex is for procreation, relaxation, pleasure and fun, expressing intimacy, or all of the above?

Ask: "What kinds of things stimulate you? Who do you want to be the initiator? How would you like me to suggest having sex? How should I tell you I'm not in the mood? How often do you think we should have sex?"

One wife, Mary Lee, said, "I always heard that the man was to be the initiator in sex. But when I asked Jim what he thought about that, he told me it would please him if I took initiative at times. It would make him feel like I desired him rather than just feeling like I was only accommodating his desires." The two of them discovered how freeing it was to talk about these things instead of having unspoken—and unmet—expectations.

7. *"What are your goals—for yourself and for us?"*

Ask your spouse what his or her dreams are. "Kevin is an incredible businessman," one wife said. "He's always been very diligent to work hard and provide well for our family. I thought he was happy until I asked him what he would do if he could do anything in the world. He said he would be in the ministry. He's now going to seminary. I'm so happy I asked him his dream; otherwise he may have stayed stuck in a job that supported us but wasn't fulfilling to him."

Helping your partner pursue her passions is vital to your marriage's health. You won't know those dreams if you don't ask.

Inquire about your spouse's goal for your marriage, too. Is it closeness? Wealth? To have a family? Career success? To be used as a team in some ministry? Discuss these dreams and set realistic goals with time limits. For example: "In five years we want to be out of debt." "In one year we want to save enough money to go on a family mission trip."

8. *"How did you communicate and resolve conflict in your family?"*

In tears, Elizabeth told her mother, "Bobby yells at me when we talk to each other." Elizabeth didn't understand how her husband could think that was okay. She was an only child who'd rarely had conflicts with her family.

Bobby, on the other hand, was the youngest of five brothers. His was a fun-loving family that spoke loudly and often. He thought he was just talking passionately to Elizabeth; she heard it as yelling.

When the two of them finally discussed their families' communication styles, they began to understand the differences. Elizabeth no longer felt "run over," while Bobby saw that his wife's low-intensity way of talking didn't mean that she was indifferent.

9. *"Are there medical issues in your family?"*

Do heart disease, diabetes, or other medical problems run in your mate's family? Is your spouse dealing with a chronic condition? How is it treated? Have there been unusual deaths in the family?

It's important to know your spouse's medical history so that you can work together to prevent further problems, collaborate on diet and exercise, and consider possible implications for your children.

As you ask these nine questions, keep your spouse's temperament in mind. If she seems hesitant to talk, don't nag. Just explain why you're looking for information and how it can bring you closer.

Remember the importance of timing, too. For example, if your mate ignored your interest in sexual intimacy last night, try waiting until neither of you is upset to discuss sexual expectations. Likewise, a spouse who's tired, stressed, or sick won't be able to focus on the issues. As for a mate who's asked about family history, she may need time to gather information—or just think.

Be considerate of your spouse's feelings. But don't neglect to ask these questions. The only way to understand your mate is to know her.

—*Sheryl DeWitt*

## TAKING IT PERSONALLY

1. Which of the nine questions are you most interested in asking? Why? Are there any questions you're reluctant to ask because you might not like the answer? If so, would it help to promise each other that the two of you will talk with a pastor or counselor if the discussion leads to conflict?

2. Rather than dumping all nine questions on your wife (or wife-to-be) at once, plan to discuss one each week for the next nine weeks. Set a time that works for both of you. Ask each other the question of the week; it shouldn't be a one-way interrogation.

# How Honest Do We Have to Be?

*11*

1. Healthy relationships are built on trust.

2. If you aren't totally honest, trust is impossible.

3. Without trust, the relationship crumbles.

This sounds simple—too simple, as it turns out.

If you're a Christian, are you required to be "absolutely" honest with your spouse? After all, the Scriptures are clear that lying is a serious affront to God. Christians are to strive for honesty—and truth is absolute, not relative.

But what does that mean when your wife asks, "Does this dress make me look fat?" What does it mean when she was intimate with a boyfriend before she met you?

In other words, does perfect honesty exist in imperfect human relationships? And if you aren't completely candid with your spouse, will your marriage fall apart?

To answer those questions, we need to ask another: What does "honest" mean?

To be honest certainly is to tell the truth. But by "honest" do you mean simply that whatever you communicate is accurate? Or do you also mean that you're obligated to communicate all information on any and all topics, both from your present and past?

Being honest in the sense of telling the truth is not the same as imparting every thought and feeling you have. Joe and Suzie learned that the hard way.

They'd been married two years. Suzie often remembered that Joe had been "honest" in telling her during a premarital counseling session that he'd had sexual experiences with two other women before becoming a Christian five years ago. He'd also told her that no children had been the result of these liaisons, and that he'd never contracted any sexually transmitted diseases.

Suzie came into the marriage a virgin, but didn't think Joe's sexual history would be a problem for her. As time went by, however, she found herself thinking more and more about these "other women" and Joe's experiences with them. She decided to be "honest" and tell her husband that she was increasingly anxious about his past dalliances. If he would just answer a couple of questions, she said, she'd be able to forget the whole thing.

Wanting to put her concern to rest, Joe reluctantly agreed to talk briefly about these old girlfriends. Suzie wanted to know their names, how they looked, why Joe was attracted to them, how long he dated them, and whether he was in love with them at the time.

He was "honest" in describing one of them as a cute, sexy blonde and the other as an attractive, more intellectual redhead. He recalled being fascinated with the redhead, and "falling in love" or at least "in lust" with the blonde. Neither relationship lasted long after a brief sexual affair.

Much to Joe's disappointment, these "honest" answers did nothing to satisfy Suzie's increasing obsession with his history. She seemed even more anxious and began to demand detailed, intimate information about the two sexual relationships. Joe began to withdraw from

Suzie's "interrogations" as he called them, and refused to talk with her about anything in his past.

Suzie, meanwhile, began to accuse Joe of hiding things from her. She said she could no longer trust him.

For Joe and Suzie, this effort to be "honest" turned into a painful, ugly series of interchanges that became toxic for their relationship, the dynamics of which remained unclear to both of them.

So is honesty the best policy?

Couples should be honest before making a lifelong commitment to marriage, disclosing information that could influence that decision. This includes medical and financial status, past marriages and children if any, spiritual journey and current walk in the faith, criminal history, and other "risk" factors.

In considering how honest to be in a marriage, though, it's important to examine the intent of the heart.

"Honesty" sounds pious, but can be a selfish excuse for meeting your own needs. In Suzie's case, one of her motives for demanding that Joe be "totally honest" was trying to relieve some insecurities. She was thinking, *How do I compare with my husband's past lovers? If I don't measure up, he'll be tempted again by another woman.* Her demand for even more intimate, detailed information became increasingly intense, resulting in a destructive process that had little to do with true honesty.

In the name of honesty, some people give their spouses too much information about past and present sinful actions and thoughts. To feel better about themselves, they dump their guilt feelings on their mates—unnecessarily hurting them.

Others have more sinister motives. Often the "honest" information being offered is carefully selected and intended to create anxiety in the spouse. For example, an insecure husband may try to create jealousy in his wife by describing how his female coworkers flirt with him.

Silence—choosing not to disclose all events of the day or all thoughts that cross your mind—isn't necessarily dishonest. In fact, sometimes the loving thing to do is to keep your mouth shut.

Giving a diplomatic answer in love rather than a cold, blunt "truth" is not the same as lying. In many instances, it's not particularly virtuous to "honestly" tell your wife that she's boring or not much of a lover.

And if she *does* ask, "Does this dress make me look fat?" the biblical admonition about "speaking the truth in love" (Ephesians 4:15) comes to mind. The flat truth is that the dress doesn't *make* her look fat. A more diplomatic and loving response than a simple "yes" is much advised. For example, you could tell her that although you think her blue dress looks better on her, she's very attractive no matter what dress she's wearing. "No, that dress doesn't make you look fat," you might say. "You look beautiful."

Being truthful in marriage is vital. But before demanding or disclosing "all," first be honest with yourself about your motives. Is this for the benefit of your partner and the relationship? Or is it really an attempt to immaturely or selfishly meet some of your own needs? Can those needs be met in a more emotionally healthy and spiritually mature way?

If you can't answer those questions, you may need help seeing the issues more clearly. In that case, consider seeking the insight of a wise spiritual leader or professional Christian counselor.

—*Phillip J. Swihart*

## TAKING IT PERSONALLY

1. When you hear that it may not be necessary to tell your spouse everything, do you breathe a sigh of relief? Why or why not?

2. Do you have more trouble with telling the truth, or with telling it in a loving way? If the former, start by telling your mate one "inconvenient truth" about yourself this week. If the latter, write down how you'll tell your mate one "uncomfortable truth" this week in words that don't accuse, mock, or devalue her.

# How Can I Get Used to Being Two Instead of One?

*12*

The sudden change that comes after the honeymoon can be one of life's most sobering moments. Some young couples describe this as "being hit in the face with a cold glass of water" or "being struck by lightning."

Others express it this way:

"I feel like I'm on another planet, and I want to go home!"

"I miss being able to do what I want to do, when I want to do it."

And here's a favorite that marriage therapists hear often: "If two becoming one means that I disappear as a person, forget it!"

If you feel like this, don't think you're alone or that your situation is hopeless. The following quotations illustrate the fact that the adjustment period from aloneness to togetherness is often complex:

> I figure that the degree of difficulty in combining two lives ranks somewhere between rerouting a hurricane and finding a parking place in downtown Manhattan.
>
> —*Claire Cloninger*

> I love being married. It's so great to find that one special person you want to annoy for the rest of your life.
>
> —*Rita Rudner*

Many couples wonder how the blending of two personalities and sets of ambitions, desires, and dreams could ever be expected by a wise and all-knowing God! Trying to adjust from "freedom" to partnership can be difficult and exasperating—but it's a process, not just a destination.

Here are two principles to remember when moving from independence to interdependence in marriage.

1. *The feelings are normal.* When we shift from being single to being married, we experience loss. Losing something leaves us feeling sad. But as we grow in our relationship with the person we committed to, the grief can turn to joy and contentment.

It's common for young couples to experience various levels of "buyer's remorse." That was the case with Nicole and Ted.

Nicole had waited for many years to find the right man to spend the rest of her life with. At age 33, she met Ted. Within 13 months they were married in her hometown of Atlanta.

Though she was certain Ted was the man God had chosen for her, Nicole missed her independence. Often she felt sad, conflicted, confused—wondering whether she'd made the wrong decision about marriage. She loved Ted and was thankful for him, realizing she couldn't have asked for a better man. But she struggled with having to give up her "alone time" and sense of freedom.

After praying, studying the Bible, and getting direction from Christian friends, Nicole began to see that her feelings were normal and that most people experience them. She accepted the responsibility of honoring the relationship God had given her with Ted. Each day she made conscious efforts to enjoy her relationship with her new husband in the fullest sense.

Though she occasionally needed time alone, Nicole learned to think in terms of two instead of one. When tempted to do her own thing at Ted's expense, she resisted. When it would have been easy to plop down on the couch after a hard day's work, she spent time with her husband first. Ted responded in a similar way, and their marriage developed into a bond filled with joy and intimacy.

That's how closeness and biblical oneness develop in marriages in spite of selfish tendencies. Though challenging and often confusing, the transition from independence to interdependence is absolutely vital to your union.

2. *It takes work to grow in oneness.* On a torn envelope, Sarah finds the following note left on the kitchen table one morning: "Sarah, I know you said you would like to spend time with me. I agree that we've really grown apart lately. I think we need to spend more time together, and I know you were looking forward to relaxing for a couple of evenings. Well, you get your wish. The boss called and said I have to work tonight.

"By the way, would you mind ironing my golf shorts when you get home? I have a tournament tomorrow. Oh, before I forget, tomorrow night the guys are coming over to watch the game. You don't mind, do you? And something else—I'm leaving on business to San Diego Monday. I'll be gone the rest of the week."

If Sarah is like most wives, she's thinking, *How in the world does this goofball think we're going to get close if he's always gone or having someone over?*

She's right; healthy relationships don't just evolve, they're nurtured.

Suppose Jesus had taken the attitude that closeness would "just happen" with his disciples. "Okay," He might say. "I have called you guys to be apostles. You have left everything to follow Me. But I have a lot of stress on Me; I have to save the world! So My 'alone time' is very important. Your job is to take the Gospel to the whole world, but I really think you can handle this without Me. I'll spend Saturdays with you, but the rest of the time you're on your own."

Is that how Jesus became "one" with His disciples? No. He understood the value of spending time with them, talking, teaching, dining, and experiencing happy and challenging moments together. There were times when Jesus needed to be alone, but He understood the value of being with His followers, too. In the end, He gave His life for them and they gave theirs for Him—the ultimate testimony of oneness.

If you find yourself struggling with the challenges of togetherness, here are some simple suggestions.

1. *Remember who brought you together.* God has united the two of you for a reason. It's no accident. He calls you to become one (Genesis 2:24), to honor one another (Ephesians 5:22-33), to love one another (1 Corinthians 13), and to remain together until death separates you (Matthew 19:9).

2. *Change the way you think.* You're still an individual. But God has called you to leave your father and mother and unite with your spouse. That means making changes in your thinking (you belong to someone else now) as well as your behavior (you don't act like a single person anymore). Changing the way you think can change the way you feel. Start thinking like a married person, and you'll probably begin to feel like one.

3. *Educate yourself about God's desire for unity in your marriage.* Read Bible passages that emphasize the importance of oneness and unity (John 17; 1 Corinthians 7). Personalize them by inserting your

name and the name of your spouse. Pray that God will show you any attitudes and actions that stand in the way of oneness. Stop focusing on your mate's mistakes, and start working on unity by changing yourself.

4. *Learn from others.* Ask couples you know who have strong marriages how they moved from independence to interdependence. What mind-sets and habits did they adopt that worked for them?

If you asked that of Bill and Ruth, here's what they might tell you.

Bill was independent. So was Ruth. For the first three years of their marriage things were so rocky that both felt they'd made a mistake in getting married. They developed separate interests and friendships, spent little time with each other, grew apart, and even considered divorce. But because of their church background, they felt they had to stay together.

Things changed on their third anniversary. They made a commitment to each other: No matter what, they would learn how to connect and develop intimacy. They began studying the Bible and praying together, and attended every marriage conference they could find. They made spending time together a hobby; where you saw one, you'd see the other. They took up golf and skiing. For the next 20 years they would have at least one date a week.

Recently Bill and Ruth went to another marriage retreat—where they were voted Most Dedicated Couple. Their switch from aloneness to togetherness hadn't just happened. They'd intentionally drawn closer and stuck with that commitment.

They'd probably tell you that intentional intimacy is an investment that always pays off—and they'd be right.

—*Mitch Temple*

## TAKING IT PERSONALLY

1. What are three things you're giving up by being married? What are three you're gaining? On balance, do you feel you're coming out ahead or behind?

2. One night this week, share a dessert with your spouse at home or in a restaurant. As you do, talk about your definitions of the following words: *independence, interdependence, aloneness,* and *togetherness.* What does sharing have to do with each of these concepts? Other than desserts, what can you share that will bring the two of you closer without "canceling out" your individuality?

# SHOULD I TELL MY WIFE ABOUT MY PAST?

## 13

If you've lived in a hot, humid climate, you probably know about cockroaches. They come out at night—and can be seen to scurry when a light is suddenly turned on.

The devil is a lot like a cockroach. He does his best work in dark places, thriving on secrets. Often when the light is turned on and the truth is revealed, he loses his power and runs.

Maybe you're harboring some secrets about your past. Does that mean you should shine the spotlight on them for your spouse? Will that make your marriage better—or worse?

There are good arguments to be made for turning on the light.

First, God's design for marriage is that couples become one spiritually, physically, and emotionally. There's a greater chance for this oneness when spouses are free from the guilt and shame that often goes with past moral failures—especially hidden ones.

Second, when two people come into a marriage with unresolved hurts or failures, it affects them as individuals. When those things are intentionally hidden, it can damage the relationship in a number of ways.

For example, let's say a wife hasn't told her husband that she was sexually abused as a child. Because of that past, she finds herself unable to be playful and relaxed in the bedroom. He begins to wonder, *Is it me?*

He starts to feel insecure about his ability to fulfill his wife sexually. *Is she comparing me to someone else?* he asks himself. He remembers her dropping a hint once that she had "a past," but refusing to share the details. His self-doubt grows.

Or the husband may have had a sexual relationship in the past. He may recall it as being more fulfilling or more exciting than what he has now with his wife. He finds himself longing for those days and that person. He begins to flirt with and fantasize about someone at work, trying to recapture the past. Not wanting his wife to know about the old affair, he refuses to talk about his feelings—and the marriage continues to erode.

In cases like these, revealing secrets from the past—especially with the help of a counselor—might be constructive.

Sometimes keeping secrets seems the safest course in the beginning, but the damage emerges later. A wife who was abused as a child might not recognize her inhibitions until after she is married and intimate. By then she fears that telling her husband will hurt their sex life further. But keeping the secret makes their relationship progressively worse.

Christian counselors differ on exactly how much of the past should be revealed to a spouse. Most would agree on the following principles, however:

1. *Honesty in a relationship is an important factor in building trust.*

2. *Detail and timing are important considerations.* For instance, a wife may benefit by knowing that her husband had sex before marriage. But knowing who, what, and where might make the information too visual and hurtful and feed the imagination in a negative

way. As for timing, secrets tend to gain momentum and strength the longer you wait to reveal them. And the sting will be far less if the method and moment of telling are carefully and considerately planned rather than impulsive or offhanded.

3. *Some things are a must to share.* Examples:

- Having had a sexual partner, no matter how ashamed you may be about it, is something that should not be hidden from a mate. It should be disclosed before marriage, especially when there is a possibility of passing on a sexually transmitted disease.

- Experiencing an abortion, sexual abuse, having a baby out of wedlock, or giving up a child for adoption can cause problems in the relationship later if they haven't already—and should be discussed.

- Legal or financial "ghosts," such as lawsuits, bankruptcies, previous marriages, and criminal charges or convictions should be revealed.

4. *When in doubt about whether to share a particular secret, get help.* It's wise to seek counsel about the potential impact of turning on that spotlight. Revealing secrets of the past can strengthen a marriage—or cause insecurity and suspicion.

5. *Search your heart and know your motive.* Do you want to reveal a secret in order to hurt your spouse? To relieve yourself of guilt or shame? To just make yourself feel better? These aren't worthy motives, especially if the cost to your mate is pain and a breach in trust.

6. *Remember that you can always confess to God—and receive forgiveness.* "If we confess our sins, he is faithful and just and will forgive us our sins and purify us from all unrighteousness" (1 John 1:9).

Still not sure what to do? Here are four questions to ask yourself before sharing your past:

- Will this make my spouse feel more secure?
- Will this let my spouse know me better?
- Will this bring us closer?
- Will this prevent problems from coming up in the future?

If you're keeping a secret, be aware that it may indicate a larger problem. You may need help to deal with shame or a lack of freedom or a need for emotional healing. You may not sense enough trust in your relationship to ensure safety from judgment or rejection.

In that case, it may be time to explore those issues with a professional counselor who can give direction. It may be better to do this *before* marriage—but it's not too late to do it now.

—*Romie Hurley*

## Taking It Personally

1. What's one thing about your past that's been fun to tell your wife or fianceé about? What's one thing you've avoided bringing up? Why?

2. If you're keeping a secret about your past, what do you think would happen if you revealed it? If you can't decide whether it would be wise to share that secret, consider asking a pastor, counselor, or other trusted mentor to help you evaluate the possible impact on your marriage.

# How Can I Adjust to My Wife's Personality?

*14*

"When she's stressed out, she talks all the time. If I get tired of talking to her after an hour or so, she gets a second wind and calls a friend!"

"He's so sensitive. I can't correct him without it making him angry. No matter what I say, he takes it wrong."

"After we leave a social event, I get so angry I can't see straight. She embarrasses me—not once, but throughout the evening."

If these statements hit home, you're not alone. Most of us have said—or at least thought—similar things about our spouses.

Couples often tell therapists that one of their toughest challenges is adjusting to a spouse's personality. Many of those people are ready to give up and resign themselves to a miserable state of existence. Others fear their situations will worsen to a point where the spouse's personality turns repulsive—and divorce will be inevitable.

So what do you do? Stay miserable? Get angry and resentful? Leave?

We suggest none of the above.

Instead, consider these facts about differences in personalities.

1. *God created us to be different.* He knew there would be a place in His plan for introverts and extroverts, for thinkers and feelers, for those who are planners and those who are spontaneous. He created

some people to be dreamers and some to be content with things as they are. "Different" doesn't automatically equal "wrong."

Proverbs 22:6 can be translated to recommend training a child "according to his bent." In other words, it's good to discover a child's distinctive personality and bring her up in a way that complements her personality instead of tearing it down. Why not apply this idea to marriages, too? Are you willing to allow your spouse the same freedom to be unique—and not the same as you?

When we realize that God planned for people to different, it's often easier to accept and adjust to a spouse's personality. It may even become possible to celebrate those differences. Otherwise, why would God create us in such variety—only to tell us to pair up and remain together for life? He's a God of compassion, not cruelty!

2. *It's easier to spot a flaw than to see a strength.* Jesus put it in terms of spying a speck in another's eye, versus seeing a log in our own (Matthew 7:3-5).

When you were dating, you probably found it easy to focus on the admirable traits of your future mate. You seemed to like the same things, enjoyed the same conversational topics, and tended to overlook each other's quirks.

Bennett, for instance, married Deb because she was such a "great communicator." Now he's annoyed because she's such a "great agitator." Dana married Marcus because he was such a "confident, strong manager." Now he's an "overconfident jerk." Juan married Paula because she was "so sweet and kind." Now he doesn't respect her because "she lets people run over her."

What changed? Why do the same personality traits we once celebrated suddenly become "logs" in our mate's eye?

During the dating process, the goal is often to conceal the "real" you and present your best side. After the wedding, the masks are dropped and unsightly reality rises to the surface. Stress, crises, pain, and disappointment also have a way of exposing what we formerly attempted to hide.

That's why it's a good idea for dating couples to go through the seasons of a year together. This allows you to see one another's imperfections. It's a test of whether you're committed enough to stay together for the rest of your lives.

"But it's too late for that," you may be saying. "We're already married!"

Then it's time to recognize the next fact.

3. *Your ability to tolerate your mate's personality changes with time.* Most of us can stand negative behavior for a while. But everyone has a limit!

Belinda, for example, could put up with Jeff's ability to make a joke out of everything—for about a year. After she became the brunt of his jokes, her level of tolerance changed. She reached a point where she despised his voice, especially his laughter.

Is that the case with you? Maybe it's not that your spouse's personality has become more of a problem; it may be that your ability to value or overlook some attributes has diminished.

Reaching your limit is no excuse for giving up on a marriage, though. Sometimes it's enough to realize that the change is in your "irritation threshold" and adjust that gauge accordingly. At other times, you may need help from a counselor to express your frustration and find a healthy tolerance level.

4. *Sometimes it's not really about personality.* Could it be that your mate has done something that deeply hurt you—and her personality has become the contention point?

That was the case with Barry. He'd always liked the fact that his wife, Wendy, was sociable and outgoing. But then he discovered that she'd been flirting with a coworker. Now Barry viewed her personality as a threat.

When your spouse hurts you, it tends to change the way you think and feel toward her. You suddenly see that person through tinted lenses, not clear ones.

If this is the case with you, healing has to occur before everyday personality issues can be objectively dealt with. Identify the real issue. Work on it—with the help of a counselor if needed. Commit to overcoming your tendency to focus on the negative aspects of your spouse's personality.

1 Corinthians 12–14 urges us to appreciate individual differences. The apostle Paul explains that every member of the "body" is valuable. Just because a part is different doesn't give us the right to despise it and set it apart from the others.

The same is true with your mate's personality. It may be different and sometimes difficult to manage. But God doesn't want this to allow division in your marriage.

One of Paul's points to the Corinthians might be summarized this way: "Learn to accept and adjust to each other, no matter what people look like or act like." That applies to husbands and wives, too.

—*Mitch Temple*

## TAKING IT PERSONALLY

1. How would you describe your bride's personality? Would you have described it that way when you first met her? If your description seems to be changing, what do you think the reason is?

2. Make a list of your partner's bothersome personality traits. Then, after each trait, write a word or phrase that describes that tendency in positive terms. For example, a "pushy" wife might also be seen as "assertive" or "having leadership qualities." An "indecisive" spouse also could be "careful" or "deliberative." How could these positive qualities, like a superhero's powers, be used "for good instead of evil" in your marriage?

# What Can I Do about Her Irritating Habits?

*15*

When you got engaged, you probably thought you were marrying the person of your dreams. After the wedding day, though, you realized your spouse had some annoying habits.

Suddenly the person who could do no wrong was in need of a makeover.

Maybe you started a reforming program, only to discover that you don't have enough resources or power to change your spouse. Now your refrain sounds something like this:

"Cathy is always late for everything. Last week I decided to go on to church without her, and then for some reason she gets mad at me!"

"Cindy never listens to me. She always interrupts me and never lets me talk. I've learned to just shut up and keep quiet."

Chances are that you married your spouse not just because you had similarities, but also for the differences. You may have been attracted to these differences because of your need to feel completed by another person. These traits may be endearing before marriage, but can disrupt the relationship afterward.

Do you have to live with these habits? Should loving this person be enough to enable you to overlook them? And if you can't, should you feel guilty?

Being annoyed by your spouse's habits is normal. The key is to learn to work together to change the habits that can be changed and learn to accept those that can't.

First, ask yourself why you want your spouse to change. Is it for your own good only? Might the change make you feel better, but cause your mate to feel imprisoned? Or is the change to help eliminate behaviors that keep your spouse from growing emotionally and spiritually? In other words, are you helping to set your partner free or just restricting her freedom?

If changing the habit would truly benefit both of you, change may be worth trying. But keep these guidelines in mind:

1. *Address the problem honestly.* "Honey, it bothers me when you gossip at the table. It teaches the children a bad habit, and it's rude and offensive to guests."

2. *Explain the benefit of change.* "Eating at the table will be more pleasant for all of us. The boys will also respect your manners and you'll be a good testimony to our guests."

3. *Don't command change.* "You're so obnoxious at the table. Stop being so catty." Instead, *request* change. Your spouse will respond more favorably.

4. *Don't attack your mate.* "You are a horrible listener. It's no wonder no one talks to you." When you attack your spouse, you crush her spirit—and don't get much cooperation. Confront the problem; don't attack the person.

5. *Discuss ways to bring about change.* Change is hard. Let your spouse know that you're on her side. Help her find ways to change those habit patterns. If the problem is overeating, for instance, go with your spouse to the gym, cook healthy meals, and go out to eat less often. Be your mate's advocate.

6. *Encourage your spouse's growth.* "You're doing a great job. I'm really proud of the effort I see. Thank you for your dedication to making this change."

7. *Recognize that change takes time.* Be patient with your spouse. Praise little steps that you see. Everyone wants to feel successful. So don't discourage your mate with comments like, "This is taking forever. How many more times do we have to deal with this?" Discouragement stunts growth, but encouragement goes a long way in motivating change. Let your spouse know you're in this together for the long haul.

8. *Focus on your spouse's good habits, not just the irritating ones.* "John makes me mad," one wife said. "I have asked him to clean the tub after each use. He never does.

"Last week when I was getting ready for work, I received a call from the hospital. John was in an accident. As I quickly dressed to go to the hospital, I noticed the dirt ring in the bathtub. I began to sob. The Lord brought to mind all the wonderful qualities of my husband, and I felt so petty for complaining about the ring in the tub. When John came home several days later, I found myself sitting in the bathroom and thanking the Lord that I would have more time with John and more rings in the tub. I was reminded of Philippians 4:8: 'Whatever is honorable, pure, just, lovely . . . think on these things.'

"When I see the ring now, I turn my thoughts to the wonderful qualities of my husband and the annoyance of that ring in the tub disappears."

9. *Pray for your spouse.* God is ultimately the one who makes change possible in any of us. So pray for your mate's efforts. And since some behaviors may never change, ask God to give you grace to accept the differences between you and your spouse.

10. *Seek to change the habit, not the person.* It's possible to help your spouse drop an irritating habit—as long as it's the habit you're trying to change. If you're trying to alter your spouse's personality or temperament, you'll be fighting a losing battle that will end in frustration for both of you.

Take Susan and Lee, for example. Susan, an extremely social person, loves to stay after church to talk, is the last to leave a party, and likes to be the center of attention. In contrast, her husband, Lee, is reserved, prefers to be in the background, and is exhausted by socializing. Lee has learned to go to parties with Susan out of love for her. But she can't expect him to become a fan of social gatherings. She needs to appreciate his willingness to go with her and not try to make him the extrovert she is.

If you follow the aforementioned guidelines and don't meet with success, it's time to ask yourself whether the battle is worth it. Some habits are so engrained that if they don't involve moral issues or character flaws, it may be best to live with them. Bringing them up repeatedly may lead only to more bitterness and conflict.

Keep praying for your spouse. And when you think of her, focus on her positive traits—instead of that irritating habit.

*—Sheryl DeWitt*

## Taking It Personally

1. How much do you think you'd have to pay your bride to give up her most irritating habit? How much would she have to pay you to ignore it?

2. If you've tried to discuss this issue before, what happened? Pick one of the ten preceding guidelines that could make a positive difference when you bring the issue up this week.

# Why Isn't Marriage the Way
# I Thought It Would Be?

*16*

On their honeymoon, Ed and Renee spent hours gazing into each other's eyes— contemplating how they'd spend their next 50 years. They decided to write those plans down as a road map for the future.

But before long, those plans hit several speed bumps.

Ed lost his job.

Renee was diagnosed with diabetes.

Habits that seemed cute at first became annoying.

When they had a son, Renee decided to stay home—which tightened the family purse strings. Ed worked more to compensate, further reducing their time together. When she voiced concern, it only seemed to irritate him.

They still loved each other. But this wasn't how either of them had written the script on their honeymoon.

You might find yourself wondering if *your* early dreams of marital bliss were more illusion than reality. Why isn't marriage turning out the way you planned?

In premarital counseling, couples often explore their expectations of marriage. But what does that mean? Are expectations the way you think your marriage *will* look, or the way you *want* it to look? The two can be very different!

People draw their marital expectations from two wells. One is courtship. If dating was wonderful and starry-eyed, why would you expect marriage to be otherwise? *If spending 20 hours a week brings us such joy,* you might think, *more time together as husband and wife could only be better!*

But think back to your courtship. Wasn't it largely a mirage?

What did you do when you didn't want to be alone? You got dressed up and did fun things together. What did you do when you were tired of talking? You went home. How did you deal with financial decisions? You made them on your own.

When you were dating, there were some built-in escape valves in your relationship. Now that you're married, there's no other home to go to. Your spouse's finances are yours, and vice versa.

By its nature, courtship allows a couple to live in denial. Marriage makes that posture much more difficult to maintain.

The other well of marital expectations is the marriage you saw firsthand when you were growing up.

That relationship provided one of two images for you to view. Either the marriage didn't seem worth duplicating, or it did.

Even if the marriage you saw was conflicted and unhappy, you may have believed things would be different for you. Without that hope, the decision to remain single would have seemed pretty appealing. But simply raising your expectations won't make your marriage better than that of your parents. You need to face past hurts and disappointments, perhaps with the help of a counselor or pastor. That may not have the same thrill that romance does, but it makes it more likely that you'll experience a fulfilling and romantic marriage.

On the other hand, you may have been fortunate enough to see a model of marriage worth replicating. For that you can rejoice! But there's a pitfall there, too. You may be locked into thinking that the way you saw Mom and Dad relate is the only healthy way for a marriage to function.

For example, let's say that your parents were both even-tempered; decisions came easily for them. You or your spouse might be more opinionated and need to discuss matters longer. That's okay, even though it's different. There are many styles in marriage that can be healthy.

Parents can affect your marital expectations in other ways, too. That was true with Tom and Jill.

Tom's expectations about marriage weren't being met. Through reading and counseling he finally recognized that those expectations were an effort to cope with a painful childhood. Growing up, he'd often been under his mother's controlling thumb. He'd brought into marriage a vow that he'd never get close enough to his wife to let her control him as Mom had. As a result, he'd never gotten close enough to truly connect with Jill.

Tom had to work through his hurts before he could begin to relate to Jill in a more meaningful way. The two of them met periodically over coffee with a seasoned couple in their church, learning what they might expect in each new stage of marriage.

They still have struggles. But Tom is learning more about God's expectations for their marriage. Unless he depends on God for the ability to love Jill, he doesn't have a prayer to make it happen. He's also learning that by staying true to his marriage, he's growing in ways he never thought possible.

Tom brought his own expectations to marriage, but God had a better idea.

If your expectations about marriage have been unrealistic, it's time to challenge them. But if you do, and still have concerns, consider the possibility that the problem might not be your expectations. You might have a problem in your marriage.

Harboring unrealistic expectations doesn't mean that everything else in a marriage is on track. Your qualms might be slightly off target, but they could be early warning signs about issues that will cause more trouble if you don't resolve them. Talk about them with your spouse in a respectful way; see whether the two of you can address them. If that fails, look to a pastor or counselor for help.

*—Glenn Lutjens*

## TAKING IT PERSONALLY

1. Would you say "the honeymoon is over" in your relationship? Why or why not?

2. Think of an older couple who could help you form realistic expectations about what might happen during the next few years of your marriage. Ask them whether they'd be willing to meet with you once or twice to describe the stages they've gone through. Then talk with your spouse about three things you can do to prepare for the likely challenges ahead.

# How Should We Divide
# Up the Chores?

*17*

When you fell in love, was the question of how to divide up the chores on your radar screen? Probably not.

But now that you're married, chores are one thing you can't escape. The daily routine for all but the very wealthy consists of activities like cooking meals, doing the dishes, washing clothes, maintaining household appliances, repairing the car(s), handling the finances, parenting the kids (if any), feeding the animals (if any), choosing insurance, and cleaning the house or apartment. Some chores pop up right after the honeymoon; others emerge over time.

It's common to think in terms of "male" and "female" chores. But should a wife automatically be in charge of shower curtains, while her husband specializes in replacing shower heads?

Christian couples may tend to think such male/female distinctions are biblical rather than traditional. But the Bible doesn't specifically support the notion that, for example, only women must cook and only men must calculate the budget and finances. After all, Jacob prepared the stew that Esau ate (Genesis 25); the "wife of noble character" in Proverbs 31 dealt with business concerns.

How you feel about dividing up chores has a lot to do with the way your parents handled this question.

Steve assumes the husband is supposed to handle all the chores outside the home and the wife handles those inside. That's the way his parents did things.

His wife, Abby, on the other hand, had a father who masterminded the family finances, vacuumed the floors, and did the gardening. She expects Steve to do the same.

Down the street, Greg recalls how his mother balanced the checkbook and painted the walls. He thinks his wife, Tyra, should follow that pattern.

Tyra, meanwhile, had a father who loved to cook. Why, she wonders, won't Greg follow in his footsteps?

Differences like these lead one spouse to feel the other isn't "pulling his or her weight" when it comes to household duties.

One young husband and wife, married only six months, came to a counselor because they'd been arguing constantly over chores. The husband was upset because his wife "wasted time" and didn't get as much done as he expected. The wife was resentful because her husband didn't feel he should have to help at home after putting in a hard day at the office.

That couple wasn't unusual. Anger and arguments over sharing responsibilities often bring spouses into counseling for resolution.

So is there a right answer to the question of dividing up chores?

A quick response might be to suggest adopting the Fox News motto, "Fair and Balanced." But what does that mean?

Here are more specific guidelines that may help prevent or bridge areas of conflict when it comes to chores.

1. *Think positively.* Most husbands and wives enter marriage expecting to share the load to some degree. Figuring out how to make the

sharing balanced and appropriate is not only desirable, but possible.

2. *Consider the rewards.* When husband and wife work outside the home, tackling chores together lifts the load. It gives you more time for individual activities. It gives you more time together.

3. *Concentrate on giftedness, not gender.* Rather than emphasizing "male" and "female" chores, talk about which jobs you enjoy or don't mind doing. Which do you have a knack for? Which would you prefer not to do?

4. *Allow for exceptions.* Helping each other out with chores during times of stress, busyness, or illness is very much appreciated by a spouse. It also tends to be reciprocated.

5. *Write it down.* Making a list of what needs to be done is essential. It's too easy to forget who's supposed to do what.

6. *Stay flexible.* No matter how fair and equal things seem at the start, you may have to make adjustments along the way. One spouse who was at home may begin a full-time job. Another may endure serious illness or injury.

7. *Don't go strictly by the numbers.* Fair and equal doesn't necessarily mean "one for you, one for me." Remember that some chores are more difficult and time-consuming than others.

8. *Chart yours, mine, and ours.* A busy, young husband and wife struggled to balance their desire for fun with the reality of day-to-day duties. They developed a simple chart that made the "to do" list look less intimidating—and more equally distributed.

MATT'S CHORES

1. Painting the house
2. Repairs on vehicles
3. Developing a budget

## OUR CHORES

1. Care for the garden
2. Cleaning the house
3. Planning vacations

## MARY'S CHORES

1. Buying groceries, fixing meals
2. Balancing checkbook
3. Home decorating

Dividing up chores is an opportunity for cooperation rather than conflict. A key to the challenge of marriage is striving to understand each other and seeking to meet each other's needs—and this is a great area in which to practice.

Even the act of discussing and dividing up what needs to be accomplished can lessen conflict. If you find yourself stuck in these issues, though, don't hesitate to seek assistance from a more experienced couple or a counselor.

—*Wilford Wooten*

## TAKING IT PERSONALLY

1. Share with your wife (or wife-to-be) how your parents divided up the following chores: taking out the garbage, cleaning the bathroom, vacuuming floors, shopping for groceries, cooking, filling out tax returns, unplugging the sink, washing clothes, changing diapers, balancing the checkbook, and attending parent-teacher conferences. What patterns were the same on both sides of the family? Which were different?

2. Make a chart like the one Matt and Mary made. Then take it a step further, discussing how often each duty needs to be performed—and under what circumstances one spouse will step in and do the other's tasks.

# WHAT IF MY SPOUSE WON'T TAKE THE "RIGHT" ROLE?

*18*

Many husbands and wives would like to "recast" their spouses in the "right" roles, as if their marriages were stage plays. These adjustments, they think, are the gateway to happiness.

"If only he would be the spiritual leader, things would be better in the house."

"If only she would cook and clean, there would be less stress around here."

The reality is that no one can force another to take on the "right" role. But the good news is that many spouses, if given the opportunity, will shoulder the necessary roles to make a marriage successful.

Two people who are truly committed to one another will do what's necessary to "fill in the gaps" in their relationship. If one is forced or nagged into assuming a needed role, though, the tendency for him or her is to lose interest in taking on the "right" part.

When Barb married Philip, she assumed that he was handy. She expected him to fix whatever needed fixing around the house or on the cars. Little did she know that Philip wasn't skilled in these areas. He'd never been shown how to do simple home or auto repairs.

She began to criticize him, which made him even more disinterested in helping. In fact, it began to disconnect him from her altogether.

Philip needed to be encouraged by his wife. He needed the time and opportunity to learn what he hadn't been taught. Instead, he felt ridiculed and hurt.

You and your spouse can avoid that pitfall by listening to each other's views on what "right" and "wrong" roles are. You'll need to do it patiently and respectfully.

Which of you should keep track of relatives' birthdays? Who should research where to send charitable donations? Which of you should take kids to the doctor, hang pictures on the walls, or ask the neighbor to turn down his music?

Only the two of you can answer those questions. But the following principles can help guide your discussion of which roles are right for you.

1. *The right role brings you together instead of driving you apart.* Remember that you're dividing responsibilities, not your relationship. It's usually not helpful to assign roles "because you're the man" or "because that's women's work," for instance. If your "one flesh" (Genesis 2:24) team is to work, you need to work together.

2. *The right role takes your strengths and weaknesses into account.* Look at each other's assets and liabilities; try to base roles on the use of strengths. For example, if one of you is more interested and more effective in maintaining a checkbook, that person should assume the responsibility.

3. *The right role allows for flexibility.* The flexibility starts during the discussion process. Try to negotiate without "hardheadedness."

Think of this as an exercise in togetherness, a way to cooperate in accomplishing vital tasks. Flexibility should continue as you carry out your responsibilities; for instance, if one spouse has handled all cooking and cleaning but takes a job outside the home, it's unrealistic to expect him or her to keep up with all the old duties as well as the new ones.

4. *The right role may be sacrificial.* There are some jobs nobody wants—but they need to be done anyway. Few of us aspire to clean the toilets, keep raccoons out of the garbage cans, or take the baby's temperature in the middle of the night. Review each other's strengths to determine which spouse comes closer to being the "expert" in an area, but don't expect an exact match. This will take humility and cooperation from both parties; if only one person (or neither) is willing to sacrifice, resentment and division will most likely make their way into the relationship. If this is the case for you, enlist a pastor or counselor to help break the stalemate.

When it comes to getting your spouse to take on a needed role, encouragement can go a long way. Cheer with your words as well as with hugs and smiles. Noticing your mate's efforts creates an atmosphere of support and teamwork.

Husbands especially need to feel appreciated, and thrive when complimented on their efforts to take on the "right" role. Wives also enjoy compliments, of course, but tend to get the most satisfaction from seeing their husbands help around the house without expecting anything in return and on their own initiative.

It's common in Christian counseling for a wife to ask, "What should I do when my husband won't assume the role of spiritual leader?" Christian husbands who avoid that role may do so because they feel anxious, self-conscious, unworthy, or overwhelmed by the prospect.

The counselor may respond with questions like these:

"How are you being a part of the solution?"

"Are you encouraging your husband, or are you nagging and putting him down because he won't assume the role?"

"When he reads Scripture, do you frequently correct him while he's trying?"

"What will happen if your husband never assumes the role?"

The answers to these questions are very important. They help the wife to focus on what can be controlled and changed.

Look for each other's spiritual strengths. Build a healthy spiritual life together. Seek guidance from your pastor as you do so. Look for a mentor whose spiritual life you admire. Make it a point to renew yourself spiritually on a daily basis, and to find new and exciting ways to bring the Bible to life for your children if you have any. Keep praying for your spouse's spiritual growth, too.

You can't *make* your spouse take on the "right" role. But you can work on the kind of relationship that makes it easier to assume the roles that are best for both of you.

That was the case with Greg and Laura, who'd just married. Both had managed their money wisely as singles; Greg liked learning about the subject, and Laura had a bachelor's degree in mathematics. She also seemed more organized about maintaining her checkbook and paid close attention to deadlines.

At first Greg wanted to be the family financial expert. Soon, though, he realized Laura was the best one for the job.

Laura, meanwhile, realized that she didn't know—or care to know—much about investing. So Greg assumed that responsibility.

This arrangement worked because Greg and Laura admitted their weaknesses and acknowledged their spouse's strengths. Their relationship allowed them to work together in the "right" roles.

Finding the "right" roles in a marriage takes honest self-assessment, time, experimentation, and a willingness to adjust. It also takes a dedication to each other that's bigger than the logistics of who does what.

*—Daniel Huerta*

## TAKING IT PERSONALLY

1. What issues regarding roles do you wish you'd discussed earlier in your relationship? Is there any reason you can't start talking about them now? Explain.

2. If you'd like your wife to take on a new role, are you willing to change yours accordingly? For instance, if you want her to take the lead in buying her next car, will you accept her choice of dealer and lender? If you want her to start making the bed, will you give up the title of "bed-making expert" and let her do it her way? How will you communicate this willingness to her?

# Do We Have to Have a Budget?

**19**

For many couples, "budget" is a scary word.

What bothers you about the idea of having a budget? Is it fear that there won't be enough money? Is it not liking to be told what to do, even by a list of numbers? Does budgeting sound too complicated?

Jennifer and Josh have been told that they ought to have a budget. They're not sure they like the idea. Here are some benefits they need to consider.

1. *A budget establishes a spending plan.* When Josh and Jennifer decide to go to a movie, it will come out of their entertainment fund—with no "guilt trip" attached. When they choose to buy a toaster, they can take money from the discretionary fund or the personal spending fund. That's because they'll have decided in advance what to do. Having a plan gives you options, and having options means freedom.

2. *A budget encourages saving.* If they follow their budget, at the end of the month Jennifer and Josh will have put $100 in savings. Without a budget, that fund may not accumulate.

3. *A budget reduces stress.* With a budget, both Jennifer and Josh will understand how much money is available each month. When

they respect the system, finance won't be a primary focus of conflict—which it often is early in marriage. As 1 Timothy 6:10 puts it, "For the love of money is a root of all kinds of evil." You and your spouse want to love each other, not money—and not allow money to cause division.

4. *A budget allows for the unexpected.* Emergency expenses can be overwhelming, especially in a new marriage. Setting aside funds for surprise expenditures can help reduce pressure on both Josh and Jennifer. Emergencies are traumatic enough without the chaos that can result from not having a "rainy day" account.

5. *A budget encourages giving.* Having a budget can help Josh and Jennifer to honor God with what's already His. Jesus said, "Do not store up for yourselves treasures on earth, where moth and rust destroy, and where thieves break in and steal. But store up for yourselves treasures in heaven, where moth and rust do not destroy, and where thieves do not break in and steal. For where your treasure is, there your heart will be also" (Matthew 6:19-21).

Budgeting that allows for generosity will help Josh and Jennifer discover how giving to God's work promotes peace and joy and enhances their closeness to Him.

6. *A budget discourages debt.* Having a plan and sticking to it will keep Josh and Jennifer from overcommitting themselves financially. Debt is a burden on any marriage. If you're in debt, formulating a plan to eliminate it could be a gift to your relationship. Crown Financial Ministries (www.crown.org) is one organization that provides advice on debt reduction as well as budgeting.

7. *A budget can be flexible.* Josh and Jennifer, like many couples, fear a budget will be a straitjacket. But financial freedom can be

expanded by constantly evaluating the budget. Maybe there's a better car insurance plan. Perhaps refinancing the mortgage to save interest is an option. Or Josh and Jennifer may want to take half the money from the "dining out" budget for the next year and put it into a "save up for vacation" account.

8. *A budget can encourage spouses to submit to the same authority—God.* To set up a budget, you have to set priorities. Discussing those and seeking God's direction in the process can go a long way toward financial harmony. If Josh and Jennifer look to God and His Word for guidance, they won't be competing to be in charge of each other's spending habits.

When you get right down to it, a budget is simply a financial plan. The budget Jennifer and Josh design will have a chance to work only if they respect each other and are willing to give up "entitlement issues." In other words, Josh can't insist on going on a hunting trip using part of the rent money. Jennifer can't buy on impulse and then accuse Josh of not making enough money.

Let's say Jennifer and Josh decide to try a budget based on their annual gross income of $46,000. Here's how they might divide their monthly expenses.

| | |
|---|---|
| Mortgage or rent | $900 |
| Utilities | $100 |
| Transportation | $140 |
| Insurance (home) | $100 |
| Insurance (cars) | $200 |
| Insurance (health) | $150 |
| Insurance (life) | $ 50 |

| | |
|---|---|
| Phone | $100 |
| Cable | $ 30 |
| Food | $300 |
| Discretionary (entertainment) | $200 |
| Personal spending | $100 |
| Giving | $300 |
| Savings | $100 |
| Emergency fund (e.g., auto repair) | $300 |
| Taxes (income) | $763 |
| TOTAL | $3,833 |

Your categories and amounts may vary. But if you want the freedom of planned spending, freedom from financial chaos in emergencies, freedom from debt, and joy in giving, a budget probably is for you.

Living on a budget means learning to live on less than your income. It may involve discipline, planning, and sacrifice. But it could be one way to experience genuine freedom on the "Monday mornings" of your marriage.

*—Betty Jordan*

## Taking It Personally

1. What scares, repels, or confuses you about budgeting? Which of the benefits listed is most convincing to you?

2. Using as a model the budget Josh and Jennifer made, prepare a monthly plan of your own. Decide how you'll keep track of how much you have left in each category—either by putting cash in envelopes representing the categories, or simply by maintaining a running tally on paper or computer. Plan to review the process in three months or less to see how it's working.

# How Often
# Is Normal?

*20*

Shifting uncomfortably at one end of the living room couch, Brady avoided the gaze of his wife, Deanna, who sat at the other end.

"I don't think I'm . . . *abnormal* to want sex several times a week," he said, keeping his voice down. "But the way you act, you'd think I was some kind of pervert."

"No, I don't think that, Brady." Deanna couldn't keep the tears from spilling down her cheeks now. "It's just that with the baby and everything, I don't have anything left to give at the end of the day."

Brady got up and started pacing in front of the fireplace, his arms extended in exasperation. "We waited to get married—and you know how hard that was. I thought once it was 'legal' we'd want to do it all the time!"

Brady and Deanna aren't the only couple clashing over the question of how often they "should" have sex. The issue usually comes up when spouses' expectations about the frequency of intercourse don't match—a common complaint.

Researchers don't all agree on how often the average couple has sex. According to *Understanding Human Sexuality* by Janet Shibley Hyde and John D. DeLamater (McGraw-Hill, 1997), the largest percentage of married couples reporting in a study said they had intercourse three times a week. But as an article on the Mayo Clinic.com Web site points out, "Statistics on sexual behavior can be quite misleading. For example, a couple might read that the average married couple has intercourse three times a week. They may not be aware, however, that this average includes a wide range. The frequency of intercourse might range from zero for some to 15 or 20 times a week for others. Therefore, even if their frequency of intercourse is more or less than three times a week, their behavior is within the range of normal human experience."

Oversimplified averages can create anxious reactions. If you have sex more than twice a week, does that make you abnormal? If you have sex twice a month, is your marriage less healthy than most?

Here are five things to remember when you and your spouse aren't sure whether the frequency of your sexual activity is "normal."

1. *Every couple is different.* Frequency of sexual activity can be a measure of the general health of a marriage. But there's no numerical standard that applies to every couple.

Factors like gender, individual expectations, developmental maturity as a couple, and cultural differences all affect the numbers. In early marriage these variables are especially evident, as the honeymoon effect wanes and we find out where our own "normal" will land on the scale.

During the first years of marriage, it's especially important to discern which sources of information about sexuality can be trusted. You can't gauge what's normal from the impressions given by many TV shows and movies, for instance. Sex also deserves the honor of privacy, which discourages comparing notes with friends on what works for them. In addition to seeking wise, godly counsel from a mentor, you might find helpful several books by Christians. You'll find some listed among the resources at the end of this guide.

2. *Quality precedes quantity.* The parenting myth of "quality time" over "quantity time" happily is being debunked. When it comes to sex, though, quality really is more important than quantity. This doesn't mean either spouse has an excuse to cop out of marital responsibilities in the bedroom. It's a call to excellence.

If you're dissatisfied with your sex life, instead of first complaining about the frequency, examine the quality. Ask yourself, "Would *I* want to be married to me?" Consider how well you meet your spouse's sexual needs; find out what changes might be in order. Once communication increases and needs are satisfied, increased frequency usually isn't far behind.

3. *There's a time to serve.* Sadly, a lot of factors in our broken world can leave one or both spouses needing special consideration. Sexual trauma, addiction, abortion, and disease affect our sexuality in profound ways. Recovery is often slow, requiring patience and understanding from both partners.

A woman's reproductive cycle also requires understanding from her husband. Premenstrual syndrome (PMS), menstruation, and pregnancy—not to mention breastfeeding and caring for infants and young children—can leave a wife drained physically and emotionally. At these times, a husband will do well to keep the "big picture" in mind, remembering that sexual intimacy may suffer temporarily—but his sacrificial service will yield fruit for the relationship in the future.

4. *Be intentional.* Impulsive, spontaneous sex can be great, but it tends to fall by the wayside as jobs, mortgages, and children enter the picture. It's certainly possible (and preferable) to keep a fun-loving

chemistry going throughout marriage, but depending on that alone is often not enough.

If you give your spouse only the leftovers of your time and energy, neither of you will be sexually satisfied. Planning a time and place for intimacy seems anything but intimate, but the lack of negotiation can lead to lack of fulfillment—or worse, to looking elsewhere for it.

5. *Sex is a picture.* Scripture paints a beautiful portrait of Christ's return for His beloved Bride, the church. Our spiritual union with Him is echoed in every aspect of our earthly marriages, including sexuality. For example, a healthy husband and wife will want to focus on the quality of their sexual relationship, not just how often they have sex. It's about the relationship—not the numbers.

It can be easy to forget that, as Brady did during that confrontation with Deanna. He remembered it later, when the two of them dropped the baby off at her mother's on the way to their weekly date.

At their favorite Italian restaurant they drifted into small talk, both regretting the earlier conflict.

"Hon, I'm sorry I raised my voice to you earlier," Brady finally blurted, then glanced around to make sure other diners weren't looking his way. "I think I've just been feeling like you don't want me like you used to. I mean, I know in my head there are other reasons. My heart just doesn't always pay attention."

Deanna fished in her purse for more tissues. "I do want to show you how much I love you," she whispered, hoping the people around her didn't notice her tears. "I get caught up in the diapers and the feedings and everything else. I'm glad we've at least got our date night to remind us to focus on us, too."

—*Rob Jackson*

## Taking It Personally

1. In a perfect world, how often would you and your wife have sex? How do you think she would answer that? If these questions are tough to answer, why is that?

2. Have you and your spouse talked about the "how often" issue? If so, who brought it up and why? If not, why not? If you need a way to bring it up, try combining it lightheartedly with a couple of other, less volatile subjects—like how often to check the oil in your car and how frequently to mop the kitchen floor.

# What If We Don't Like the Same Things Sexually?

*21*

Jill didn't know what to say when she opened Mark's gift. The pretty package had been a total surprise. "It just made me think of you," he'd told her.

Judging by the size of the box, she'd thought it might be a new scarf or a sampler of chocolates. The last thing she'd expected was this lace teddy.

Didn't Mark know she wasn't the lingerie type? She could imagine how big her thighs would look in this thing.

Sometimes she thought they'd never see eye to eye when it came to sex. They'd been married only a year, and already their differences were clear. What would things be like five years from now—if they made it that far?

Jill and Mark are learning to their chagrin that sexual arousal is a very individual matter. One spouse wants the lights on; the other wants it dark. Each partner prefers a certain touch, a certain time, even a certain temperature.

When you and your mate like "different strokes," what should you do? Here are five suggestions.

1. *Discover your comfort zone.* You probably would expect to negotiate which colors to paint the rooms of your new house, or

whether to serve tofu for dinner. Why be surprised if you encounter some differences in your sexual desires? As you discover your "comfort zone" as a couple, keep in mind that this process is a normal developmental task for every marriage.

Some argue that this process could be helped along by living together before the wedding. But statistics prove otherwise. Studies reveal that, instead of increasing sexual compatibility, premarital cohabitation actually boosts the likelihood of sexually transmitted disease, sexual dysfunction, codependency, divorce, and loss of trust. Clearly, becoming one flesh is sacred for a reason.

2. *Be a servant.* Your approach to sex should mirror your approach to marriage in general: "Serve one another in love" (Galatians 5:13).

Solomon referred to his wife as "my sister, my bride" (Song of Solomon 4:10). Can you keep the perspective of being brother and sister in Christ as well as being spouses? A servant's attitude can guard against letting differences in bed become a power struggle or cause for resentment.

Basic issues of preference, such as whether to have the lights on or which positions are more pleasurable, are good opportunities to listen and learn what pleases your spouse. If something causes one partner embarrassment or discomfort, he or she should never feel pressured to participate. It's also important that both partners express preferences without criticism and without judging each other.

3. *Discern moral issues.* Each of us enters marriage with an "arousal template" or set of stimuli that triggers sexual interest. If you've had prior sexual relationships or exposure to pornography, for example, unhealthy appetites may have been added to your template.

Even between consenting spouses, certain sexual behaviors are still wrong. For example, a husband may claim that pornography helps his sex life—but its use actually constitutes an act of adultery (Matthew 5:27-28). Any sexual practices that are demeaning or physically harmful will damage true intimacy as well as violate biblical guidelines. Work together to find *what's* right instead of fighting over *who's* right.

4. *Address trauma or addiction.* If conflict over sex escalates beyond simply choosing a "menu" you both like, it's possible there's a history of sexual trauma for one or both spouses. Associating shame or fear with sexuality is a powerful dynamic to overcome. Severe trauma can produce a condition known as Sexual Aversion Disorder. Survivors of childhood sexual abuse often need the help of a professional Christian counselor to restore a healthy sex life.

Addiction to pornography, fantasy, and masturbation can put another big roadblock in a couple's path. Seeing sex as forbidden, dirty, or provocative leads to unhealthy fixations. A spouse may feel the addict is "not really there" during sex or that he or she is being used as a sexual object rather than loved intimately. Childhood sexual trauma is a frequent precursor to pornography addiction, and professional therapy is a critical tool for recovery.

5. *Talk about sex.* No matter what your sexual differences are, the first step to connecting well sexually is to do so verbally. Sometimes discussing these issues during intimacy can evoke feelings of shame or embarrassment. So it's often a good idea to wait and discuss it later, outside the bedroom.

Once you've established a healthy pattern of communication, conversation can even contribute to the sexual experience. You and your spouse can connect physically and at deeper levels as well. Talking about your love and desire for your spouse will build a safe, satisfying experience for both partners before, during, and after sexual intercourse.

Let's get back to Jill and Mark. Jill's still standing there with the gift of lingerie. What should she do?

Mark hesitates, seeing her expression. "I—I hope I didn't shock you with the present," he stammers. "I know it's not your usual style, but I really thought you'd look beautiful in it."

Jill smooths the gold ribbon on the box. She starts thinking about how Mark has shown her in so many ways that she is God's gift to him.

A shy smile plays across her lips. She even quits worrying about how her thighs would look in this outfit.

*Okay,* she thinks. *As long as he treasures me like this, I'll wrap his gift any way he likes.*

—*Rob Jackson*

## TAKING IT PERSONALLY

1. If you're not married yet, does the possibility that you'll have to work out your sexual differences after the wedding make you nervous, or sound like a good chance to get closer? Why?

2. If you're married, what differences have you noticed in the ways you and your wife approach sex? Have you talked about this? If so, what happened? If not, it may be easier to bring up the subject if the two of you first read the Song of Solomon from the Bible. See whether you can find at least half a dozen possible references to lovemaking, and talk about whether those "techniques" appeal to you.

# Why Don't We Speak the Same Language?

*22*

Are men and women really from different planets?

Any marriage counselor can provide tons of examples of husbands and wives who, having lived together for 20 or 30 years (let alone just 4 or 5), are in some ways a complete mystery to each other. The obvious answer is that God chose to wire males and females very differently. Some would even suggest that this illustrates His sense of humor.

It's possible that the communication gender gap lies in how messages are perceived. But the style and content of the messages themselves differ, too. Men tend to use language to transmit information, report facts, fix problems, clarify status, and establish control. Women are more likely to view language as a means to greater intimacy, stronger or richer relationships, and fostering cooperation rather than competition.

In other words, it's "debate vs. relate." That means you and your spouse may be tuned in to very different "meanings" in what each of you is saying. This provides fertile ground for misunderstanding, hurt feelings, and conflict. What one of you thinks is the other's "hidden meaning" can be 180 degrees out of phase with what the speaker really intends to communicate.

This can easily lead to distorted conclusions about the other person's motivations.

*She's an unreasonable, demanding nag who won't leave me alone to watch the football game,* he thinks.

*He's an insensitive, domineering bore who doesn't have a clue about my feelings and doesn't want one,* she tells herself.

Nancy and Ralph are having this kind of conflict.

Nancy sits in the counselor's office in tears. Ralph, her husband of three years, sits stony-faced, two feet away on the same couch, his arms crossed over his chest. The atmosphere is thick with her fury and his defiance.

She begins the session with a litany of Ralph's alleged failures, the worst being his neglect of her needs. He is, she says, "never home." Self-employed, he works long hours and takes frequent business trips. Sometimes he leaves on the refrigerator lists of things for her to get done while he's gone. He also leaves her with the care of a one-year-old.

When he's home, she says, he's either restoring an antique car or wanting to jump into bed for a quick sexual romp—for which he seems to have plenty of energy. When she's dead tired and turns him down, he pouts and sometimes storms out to the garage and his beloved Chevy. She notes with undisguised sarcasm that he's always too tired to just talk to her.

The final straw: Last week, on her birthday, he was gone on another business trip. She feels abandoned and unloved.

When Ralph finally speaks up, it's to say that things are usually much more peaceful in the garage than in the bedroom. At least the Chevy doesn't treat him like he's some dirty old man.

He can't understand why Nancy is so angry about his long hours at work. She seems to him to have no concept of what it takes to earn the money needed each month to pay the bills. This is how a husband and father takes care of—loves—his family. And why would she be upset about his efforts to organize on a list the chores that need to be done when he's out of town?

When she caustically remarks that she isn't one of his employees, it makes no sense to him. What does that have to do with their family life? Of course he loves her, he says. Look at everything he does to be a good husband.

Standing outside looking in, it seems easy to see that when it comes to understanding each other's languages, Nancy and Ralph are missing each other by a mile. In many respects, they exemplify stereotypical male-female struggles with differences in communication.

Of course, one size never fits all. Females don't all fit neatly into one communication-style box and males into another. Some men can be quite nurturing and emotionally empathic in their language; some women are aggressive and task-oriented in theirs.

Still, you needn't be surprised if you and your spouse sometimes seem to need a translator. In his book *How Do You Say "I Love You"?* (InterVarsity Press, 1977), Dr. Judson Swihart notes, "Often the wife comes in [to the marriage] speaking French and the husband speaking German—in an emotional sense. Unless you hear love expressed in a language that you can understand emotionally, it will have little value." The author goes on to say, "Fi uoy era gniog ot etacinummoc na edutitta fo evol drawot ruoy esuops, you must learn to speak his or her language."

It's hard to do that if, like too many couples, you enter marriage focused on being loved rather than on giving love. Try making it your goal not to change your spouse but to adapt to her style of communication. Turn your attention to hearing the heart of your partner rather than to the frustration you may feel about not being heard or understood.

If you feel stuck, and that your marriage is in a hole that just gets deeper, do something about it. Make a date with each other once a week to try a communication exercise. For example, the wife talks for ten minutes about feelings or issues she has; the husband does nothing but listen. He may respond only with, "I don't understand; could you restate that?" or "What I hear you saying is . . ."

Then he talks for ten minutes and she listens. She can ask only for clarification or affirmation that she's hearing him accurately.

At the end of the exercise, neither of you is allowed to try to "straighten the other one out," react angrily to something you didn't want to hear, or debate the issue. During the next such "date," the husband will talk first and the wife second.

Other approaches to getting "unstuck" include attending a well-recommended weekend Christian marriage retreat, participating in a couples' support group through your church, or enlisting the help of a licensed Christian marriage counselor.

This is not a hopeless situation. In fact, compared to many marital conflicts, it's a state that can more quickly and remarkably improve—when two children of God who are committed to their marriage decide to work on it and seek appropriate help.

*—Phillip J. Swihart*

## TAKING IT PERSONALLY

1. On a scale of one to ten, with ten highest, to what degree do you and your bride (or bride-to-be) fit the "debate vs. relate" pattern? How have differences in your communication styles affected your relationship so far?

2. Try the communication exercise described in this chapter. For ten minutes, tell your partner about feelings or issues you have; she listens, responding only with, "I don't understand; could you restate that?" or "What I hear you saying is . . ." Then she talks for ten minutes and you listen, asking only for clarification or affirmation that you're hearing her accurately. Neither of you is allowed to try to "straighten the other one out," react angrily to something you didn't want to hear, or debate the issue. During the next such "date," your partner will talk first, you second.

# Is It Okay to Fight?

*23*

In a word, no.

That assumes "fighting" isn't just disagreeing and expressing negative emotions. Those things are inevitable in a marriage. But if fighting is trying to resolve those feelings and problems through abusive behavior, it's unhealthy.

Conflict occurs when two people have a difference of opinion that hasn't been resolved. This can happen when you and your spouse disagree over where to go for dinner, whose family to spend the holidays with, or what each person's chores were this week. All of these are normal marital conflicts that can be worked out.

When arguments turn into verbal or physical abuse, though, it isn't healthy for any marriage. If you consistently attack your spouse with statements like, "I'm sorry I married you," "You are so stupid," and "I hate you," you've moved from arguing to abusing.

If you throw things at your spouse—pillows, silverware, pictures, vases—it only leads to more conflict and hurt. And you *never* hit, push, shove, kick, or spit at your spouse. This is physical abuse. Not only is it immoral and illegal, but it causes tremendous damage to your relationship. If this is the way you deal with conflict, you need to seek counseling to learn appropriate ways to reconcile.

Those appropriate ways don't include simply submerging your

differences instead of dealing with them honestly. Many couples try to sidestep or hide their conflict because disagreements can be painful. That leads some spouses to think their own arguments are abnormal.

"I never see other couples fight," Gary told a friend. "It makes me feel like Katie and I have a bad marriage." Gary doesn't realize that some couples share their conflicts openly, while others are more private. Some couples appear to have no conflicts, but in time they often have distress in their marriages because they had just internalized conflict and allowed hurt and resentment to build. Their anger may explode, doing incredible damage to the relationship.

A husband we'll call Paul was one who tried to suppress conflict because he feared fighting. "I fell in love with Lucy because we never fought before we got married," he told his accountability group. "I am so afraid of divorce because of my parents. They fought all the time and look where it led them. If Lucy and I continue to fight, I'm afraid we'll end up like my folks."

Contrary to what Paul believed, divorce is most common when conflict is hidden or unresolved—not when it's dealt with openly. Conflict in itself doesn't lead to divorce. Lack of resolution has brought divorce at worst and unhappy marriages at best.

Conflict resolution may sound complicated, but it's possible. It's a skill that requires the commitment of both spouses and can be refined with practice.

Here are 10 things to remember about resolving conflict without fighting.

1. *Deal with disagreements as soon as possible.* Confront issues as they arise. The longer a conflict stews, the larger the issue becomes;

time tends to magnify a hurt. As the Bible says, "Do not let the sun go down while you are still angry, and do not give the devil a foothold" (Ephesians 4:26).

2. *Be specific.* Communicate clearly what the issue is. Don't generalize with words like "never" or "always." When you're vague, your spouse has to guess what the problem is. Try something like, "It frustrates me when you don't take the trash out on Mondays," rather than, "You never do what you say you're going to do."

3. *Attack the problem, not the person.* Lashing out at your spouse leaves her hurt and defensive. This works against resolving conflict. Your goal is reconciliation and healing in your relationship. Let your mate hear what the problem is from your point of view. Say something like, "I'm frustrated that the bills didn't get paid on time," instead of, "You're so irresponsible and lazy. You never pay anything on time."

4. *Express feelings.* Use "I" statements to share your understanding of the conflict: "I feel hurt when you don't follow through." "It makes me angry when you tease me in front of your friend." Avoid "you" statements like, "You're so insensitive and bossy."

5. *Stick with the subject at hand.* Most people can deal with only one issue at a time. Unfortunately, many spouses bring two or three issues to an argument, trying to reinforce their point. This confuses the confrontation and doesn't allow for understanding and resolution. It's better to say, "It hurt my feelings when you didn't include me in your conversation during dinner with our friends," rather than, "You never include anyone, you always think of yourself. Whenever we're with other people, you always ignore me. Everyone thinks you're selfish."

6. *Confront privately.* Doing so in public could humiliate—or at least embarrass—your spouse. This will immediately put her on the defensive and shut down any desire to reconcile.

7. *Seek to understand the other person's point of view.* Try to put yourself in your spouse's shoes, an exercise that can lead to understanding and restoration. That's what Mia was doing when she told her sister, "Jeff had a hard day at the office today. His boss chewed him out. That's why he's quieter than normal, so I didn't take it personally. I know when I've had a hard day, I need time for myself, too."

8. *Set up a resolution plan.* After the two of you have expressed your points of view and come to an understanding, share your needs and decide where to go from here. That might mean saying something like, "In the future, it would help to discuss with me how we'll spend our savings—rather than telling me after the fact."

9. *Be willing to admit when you're wrong.* Sometimes a conflict occurs because one person's behavior was inappropriate. Be willing to confess and ask forgiveness from your spouse if you've wronged her. That process can help to heal the damage in your relationship. Try something like, "I'm sorry I was unkind to you. Will you please forgive me?" If you're the offended spouse, be gracious enough to accept your spouse's apology.

10. *Remember that maintaining the relationship is more important than winning the argument.* Winning an argument at the expense of losing the relationship is a defeat for both of you. Finding a solution that benefits both spouses lets everybody win.

What if the two of you just can't seem to find that solution? When you can't get past a specific conflict, seek the help of a counselor.

Fighting isn't healthy, but conflict isn't always bad. In fact, it can be a tool for strengthening relationships. When conflict is handled correctly, two people share their hearts with each other, trying to listen and be heard while connecting on a deep level.  When you deal with conflict in a caring and positive way, the result can be a deeper relationship and greater intimacy.

"In your anger do not sin" (Ephesians 4:26). God knew that we'd have anger and conflict in our relationships. But anger isn't a sin as long as we seek to resolve the conflict.

"If it is possible, as far as it depends on you, live at peace with everyone" (Romans 12:18). Instead of fighting, are you doing your part to reconcile and restore your relationship with your mate?

—*Sheryl DeWitt*

## Taking It Personally

1. How do you and your bride (or bride-to-be) define "fighting"? How would each of you answer the question, "What was your first fight?"?

2. As individuals, make lists of the "10 things to remember about resolving conflict without fighting." But put them in the order reflecting how important you believe they are. Then compare results. Next, give yourselves 10 minutes to reach consensus as a couple on the order of the listed items. Be sure to follow the 10 "rules" as you have your discussion.

# How Can We Work Out Disagreements?

## 24

Whether you've been married five years or engaged for five days, you've had disagreements with your bride (or bride-to-be). *Having* them is not the issue. The real issue is whether you can deal with them in a healthy way. Destructive patterns of disagreement can leave behind emotional scars that never heal.

Most couples think their clashes are unique, but conflict has been around since Adam and Eve. Instead of learning from our ancestors' mistakes, though, we tend to copy them. If Mom screamed and threw CorningWare at Dad when she was angry, daughter will tend to do the same in her own marriage. If Dad withdrew by watching TV every time conflict arose, son will be inclined to follow his example.

No matter what was modeled by your parents, however, you can reframe your thinking. You can realign the way you handle disagreements to better reflect the pattern God wants to see.

Can you imagine Jesus dealing with disagreements as we often do with our spouses? How would He feel about the way you treat your mate during a heated argument?

"But that's just the way I am," you might say. "Besides, my spouse keeps provoking me!" Instead of justifying our behavior, we need to discover how to properly react to disagreements no matter how intense they may be or who's at fault.

Each time you work out a disagreement in a healthy way, you're better equipped to deal with the next one. Conflict handled properly can fine-tune a relationship: "As iron sharpens iron, so one man sharpens another" (Proverbs 27:17).

Resolving disagreements can also "unstick" a couple, moving the two of you to new levels of intimacy and growth. Some of the closest moments a couple can experience often arrive after resolving conflicts. It's like a lightning storm on a warm summer night; though the lightning itself may be scary, it helps to clean the air. Negatively charged ions produced by the storm attach themselves to pollutants, which fall to the ground. That's why the air smells so clean at those times.

The same is true when you deal with disagreements in an appropriate way. Even if the discussion is loud and animated, it can help to rid relationships of contaminants and move you in a positive direction.

To understand how to handle disagreements effectively, let's first look at some techniques that *don't* work.

1. *Denial.* Why are so many married women in our society depressed? Quite a few psychologists believe it's because they don't feel free to discuss frustrations and disagreements with their husbands. That's because husbands tend to deny such problems and refuse to confront them.

Some men simply don't know how to deal with disagreements properly, but many have discovered a payoff in not resolving conflict. They can maintain control by refusing to discuss problems, keeping their wives guessing about the state of their relationship. Wives then hold back because they've discovered that keeping peace with their husbands keeps the men in a good mood and increases the chances of intimacy.

This is not a healthy approach. Failing to resolve disagreements affects our relationships as arthritis does our bodies; it impairs movement, slows us down, and causes a lot of pain. The only way to deal with "relational arthritis" is to develop healthy responses to conflict.

2. *Downplaying.* This is the "Oh, it's nothing" response. This often happens when you feel that dealing with the issue is an exercise in futility. You tell yourself that things will only turn out like before—with your spouse not listening and with both of you upset.

But downplaying the significance of a problem doesn't make it go away. It only sets a negative precedent for dealing with future disagreements.

3. *Exaggeration.* Don't make a disagreement bigger than it is. Not every minor irritation and difference in perspective has to be dissected and "put to rest." Does it really matter if your spouse doesn't share your enthusiasm for sweet pickles and the Three Stooges? Does either of you have to win a debate over which brand of paper towel or route to your church is best?

4. *Nagging.* Don't fall prey to the idea that picking a fight is the best way to get your spouse's attention and deal with a disagreement. Constant nagging is a common example of such erroneous thinking.

A dad was watching the Atlanta Braves on TV one day when his four-year-old came up and wanted to wrestle. Just to see how the boy would respond, the father ignored him and stared at the game. The child made faces, waved, and jumped up and down, but Dad gave no response. Finally the boy knocked on his father's forehead and asked, "Hey, Dad, are you in there?"

Lesson: It's better to do a little gentle "knocking" than to incite a riot to get your mate's attention. "A gentle answer turns away wrath, but a harsh word stirs up anger" (Proverbs 15:1).

5. *Resurrecting the dead.* Bringing up lifeless issues from previous disagreements only "stirs the stink." Perhaps that's why the apostle Paul wrote that love "keeps no record of wrongs" (1 Corinthians 13:5).

When a disagreement is over, it's over! Don't rehash old arguments. Some counselors suggest that couples shouldn't bring up an issue that's more than a month or two old. In other words, don't get *historical* in your marriage by continually bringing up the past!

So much for the don'ts. Here are some positive ways to deal with disagreements in your marriage.

1. *Pick the right time and place.* Get away from the telephone, TV, pager, e-mail, and other distractions. Pick a soothing, peaceful environment; a Saturday shopping trip at Sam's Club isn't a good time or place to resolve conflict! Neither are moments when you're going out the door, sitting down to dinner, or lying down for a good night's rest.

Be willing to say, "I agree that this is important, but we need to wait till later to talk about it. Let's go out tomorrow night." Allowing 24 hours to cool down and think is often a wise alternative anyway.

2. *Be prepared.* Understand that emotional events like birthdays, weddings, holidays, anniversaries, and graduations are a natural breeding ground for disagreements. People tend to be "wired and tired"; little sparks can ignite big fires. Try to get plenty of rest before these events, and give your spouse extra grace and forgiveness.

3. *Talk about yourself.* When discussing disagreements, learn to use "I" statements such as "I think" or "I feel"—rather than "you say" or "you always . . ." "You" accusations are usually meant to hurt, not to bring peace and understanding.

4. *Listen more than you talk.* Seek to understand where your partner is coming from, even when you may not agree with her viewpoint. Learn to listen instead of just trying to figure out what you're going to say next.

Temper and control what you think you have a right to say, too. As Ogden Nash put it, "To keep your marriage brimming with love in the loving cup, whenever you're wrong, admit it; whenever you're right, shut up."

5. *Keep your fingers to yourself.* Pointing fingers may be acceptable when correcting toddlers or pets, but it's not healthy between spouses. Pointing is a form of attacking, indicating that the recipient has done something terribly wrong—which often isn't the case. And no one, including your spouse, likes to have a finger wagged in her face.

6. *Keep your arguments out of the bedroom.* That's a place for unity and intimacy, not hashing out differences. Don't use sex (or lack thereof) to manipulate your partner. Sex was never designed to be used as a weapon, withheld without mutual consent (1 Corinthians 7:3-5).

7. *Remember that it's your problem, too.* It's tempting to say, "I don't have the problem, you have the problem!" But if there's trouble in your relationship, it belongs to both of you!

You're a vital part of a *marriage system.* When one part of the system is out of kilter, it throws the entire system off balance. It's like touching a mobile hanging over a baby crib; disturb part of it, and you affect the whole thing.

When you view your spouse's problem as your own, you're much more likely to get serious about helping to work it out. This makes a "double-win"—rather than an "I win, you lose" scenario—more likely.

8. *Learn to see through conflict.* Search for the real issues that often lie beneath the surface. Say, "Wait a minute. We keep arguing about all kinds of irrelevant stuff. What's the *real* problem here?"

9. *Bring God into the conversation.* Ask Him for wisdom when you can't seem to find the answers (James 1:5-6). And if the two of you are Christians, nothing will put a heated argument on "pause" more quickly than two small words: "Let's pray!"

10. *Remember your vows.* Don't threaten divorce during conflict. Threats will only intensify the pain—and leave scars. "For better or worse" will not be stricken from your vows simply because you're in the middle of a major disagreement.

Are you and your spouse disagreeing? Look for mutually beneficial solutions that resolve the tension. If the conflict is too intense to handle, or if one spouse gets extremely emotional, call a time-out until you've both calmed down. If that doesn't help, involve a counselor to assist you in getting perspective.

You can't eliminate disagreements in your relationship. But by taking a proactive approach early in your marriage, you can learn to address conflict in a way that makes everyone—including the Lord— smile.

—*Mitch Temple*

## Taking It Personally

1. How did your parents deal with conflict when you were growing up? How did your mate's parents handle it? How do these models compare with the way you'd like to handle it in your marriage?

2. Which of this chapter's five "techniques that don't work" have the two of you tried? What happened? Which of the ten positive suggestions will you put into practice next time you face a disagreement? What's a signal (for example, pointing to your eyes to symbolize "Learn to see through conflict") that will help remind you to do that?

# Do I Have to Forgive
# My Wife?

## 25

The short answer, if you're a Christian, is yes.

Jesus Christ has been crystal clear on that subject: "And when you stand praying, if you hold anything against anyone, forgive him, so that your Father in heaven may forgive you your sins" (Mark 11:25).

The apostle Paul echoes this idea: "Bear with each other and forgive whatever grievances you may have against one another. Forgive as the Lord forgave you" (Colossians 3:13).

Short answers to profound questions, however, are not always completely satisfying. On the surface, they seem to gloss over the complexities.

After all, some offenses are so grievous that it's difficult to *want* to forgive a person who's betrayed your trust and her vows to God—much less actually *do* so. Putting things in perspective, of course, most offenses in marriage don't rise to that level of pain and destructiveness.

Both Jesus and Paul answered this question by emphasizing that the most important reason to forgive is that we've been forgiven. If we've asked for God's forgiveness through Jesus' sacrifice, for our terribly long list of offenses against Him (and if we think we haven't offended Him, we're really out of touch with reality), He's already forgiven us. Why would we do less for those—including our spouses—who have wronged us?

Another good reason for forgiving a spouse is that it's in your own best interest to do so. As in art, what isn't positive space is negative space. What's left if we decide not to take the positive step of forgiving? The negatives of depression, anger, self-pity, and bitterness will be fertilized.

Not to forgive is costly—to the person who chooses not to do so, and to those around that person—even more than to the target of the person's chronic wrath.

Some husbands and wives seem highly invested in keeping minutes of all past sins and offenses of their spouses. *Ka-ching, ka-ching, ka-ching*—the cash register of marital history just keeps adding up the injustices, great and small, perceived and real.

One day that gunnysack of unforgiven hurts becomes so heavy that the aggrieved spouse, irritated by some insignificant infraction, feels the irresistible urge to dump them on the other's head. The pent-up poison of accrued bitterness blows out like a volcanic eruption. The recipient feels righteously indignant that a major injustice, a massive overreaction to nothing, has been perpetrated on him or her. This exchange, born of many choices not to forgive, solves nothing, resolves nothing, heals nothing.

Failing to forgive also gets a relationship stuck in an unending, repetitive cycle of blaming each other—rather than taking responsibility for one's shortcomings. This is a no-growth, slow-death strategy, again filling what could be positive space with negative space, which can doom marriages. It's also a terrible model for children to follow and to pass on to future generations.

But what about offenses that seem almost unforgivable? What about a father who sexually abuses his children, or an unrepentant wife who flaunts a lesbian affair? How do you forgive that?

Ultimately, forgiveness is an attitude—one that may be understood only by you and the Lord. It's giving up your insistence on getting revenge. It is not sweeping a crime under the rug or denying the enormity of what an offender has done.

In the case of abuse, your first action may need to be ensuring your safety and that of your children, if any. Forgiving a violent or perverted spouse is not the same as being naïve or stupid about his or her potential to do further harm.

Forgiveness is also not equivalent to forgetting a spouse's track record. It doesn't mean that an abusive husband or wife will be immediately allowed back into the family home after a quick, superficial, even tearful "repentance." It doesn't mean that an unfaithful spouse must be welcomed back without a commitment to counseling and behavior change.

There are times, for example, when a wife is afraid to forgive her serially adulterous husband for fear that he'll only betray and hurt her again. Her instincts may be exactly right; he'll be chasing another skirt within a month. Forgiving him does not mean that she must permit him to continue his sinful lifestyle and remain in a sham marriage to her.

One husband, Brent, began "staying late for work." His wife, Shannon, happened on a cell phone bill that included many calls to one number she didn't recognize. Some of these calls were made late at night and on weekends. When she called the number, a woman who turned out to work in Brent's office answered.

This all seemed heartbreakingly familiar to Shannon. Brent had been involved in two affairs—that she knew of—during their marriage. This was number three. The old feelings of hurt, betrayal, and anger came flooding back.

In the past, Brent had been very "repentant" when caught. She thought she'd forgiven him. Now she wasn't so sure. The only certain thing was that she wasn't about to forgive him again; she'd had it.

If you're at the edge of this cliff, married to an abusive spouse or a mate who's continued to trash you and your marriage vows through sexual infidelity, seek the help of a pastor or Christian marriage counselor.

If the situation isn't that grave, but you harbor an unforgiving spirit and find it impossible to let go, ask God to give you the power to *want* to forgive. Then commit yourself to doing so.

"But what good will that do?" you might ask.

First, it will restore your fellowship with God that may have been quenched due to this issue in your spiritual life.

Second, it will open the door—at least in relationships that haven't been irretrievably damaged—to the possibility of healing and restoration with your spouse. It may bring greater intimacy than you've had in a long time.

Finally, it can bring freedom from the bonds of resentment, allowing emotional health—perhaps even better physical health. It can build a greater sense of joy and peace to fill that negative space in your life—and displace the occupant of bitterness.

*—Phillip J. Swihart*

## TAKING IT PERSONALLY

1. How often do you tend to empty the "gunnysack of grievances" you have against your bride (or bride-to-be)? Would you recommend this approach to other grooms? Why or why not?

2. If you struggle to forgive something your partner has done, is it time to talk with a pastor or counselor about the situation? What do you think will happen if you don't? If you fear that forgiving your partner will only encourage her to continue hurting you, how could a counselor help to keep that from happening?

# How Can I Get Her to Forgive Me?

## 26

Rebecca and Mark stood in the church office after worship service. They were arguing about a topic that had surfaced during the sermon: forgiveness.

Mark couldn't seem to refrain from bringing Rebecca's mistake up again. Nine months ago, while Mark had been away on an extended business trip, she'd contacted an old boyfriend simply because she was lonely and curious about what he was doing these days.

Nothing else had occurred between the two. But when Mark had found the guy's number on her cell phone bill, he'd imagined the worst.

Rebecca had been penitent and tearful. She'd realized it was inappropriate and had asked Mark more than once to forgive her. But he seemed unable to do that.

Now they stood in the church office, clashing again over the incident. Almost everyone had gone home after the service.

James, an older deacon, could tell the young couple was having a fight as he walked by the office's glass door. After several moments he approached the pair and asked whether they were okay.

They said they were, but admitted something had come up

during the sermon that exposed old wounds. James figured it was connected with forgiveness.

"You know," he said, "when my wife and I were first married, I did something stupid which I regretted a long time. And though she is now gone on, she did something that I will never forget. She taught me a lot."

He gently placed his hand on Mark's shoulder. "If I can help you," James added with tenderness, "let me know. I will be praying for you." Then he walked away.

Curiosity got the best of the couple. That evening, Mark called James and asked if he and Rebecca could drop by Tuesday evening to hear the rest of the story. James quickly agreed.

After Mark and Rebecca arrived at the little house, James asked them to tell him a little about their problem. After several minutes of listening, he began to relate his own story.

While serving in the Korean conflict, James had been unfaithful to his wife. Overcome with shame, he'd confessed his sin to her the evening he returned from duty.

For the next several months, James worked to earn back his wife's trust. After proving his love through many difficult days, he received a special gift from her.

Now James pulled a piece of yellowed paper from his Bible and handed it to Mark. On it was the following:

"Let all bitterness, and wrath, and anger, and clamor, and evil speaking, be put away from you, with all malice: And be ye kind one to another, tenderhearted, forgiving one another, even as God for Christ's sake hath forgiven you" (Ephesians 4:31-32, KJV).

Under the Scripture passage was written the following: "James, I forgive you. If I were in your shoes, I may have done the same thing.

God burned this verse on my heart and I have obeyed. You have proven yourself worthy of forgiveness and through the months I have learned how to forgive you. I love you and believe in you. Forever yours, Sue."

James wiped one lonesome tear from his eye. "The gift she gave me was forgiveness," he said. "I hope you two will learn to forgive each other like my wife did for me."

That night changed Mark and Rebecca forever. Though they both came from homes where forgiveness was sparse, they committed to learn how to forgive and be forgiven.

Like Mark and Rebecca, most couples struggle with learning how to forgive. It's not something that comes naturally for us; it's something we learn to do. Jesus must have known that when He commanded us to pray for our enemies. He knew it wouldn't happen by itself, but that a directive was needed.

Is your spouse having a hard time forgiving you? There are some things you can do to help.

1. *Recognize that forgiveness is a process.* It ebbs and flows; it starts, stops, and starts again; it gets better and gets worse. No matter what the issue is that caused your spouse to be hurt, forgiveness can be more than just a one-shot decision. Understand that forgiving you may take time.

If your mate occasionally seems to struggle with or dwell on what you did, that doesn't necessarily equal a refusal to forgive. Sights, sounds, and memories can trigger an episode of struggle. If you're impatient or inconsiderate, it will only cause more hurt. Pursue understanding, not just the desire to put the conflict behind you.

2. *Realize that fear can be a barrier to forgiveness.* Fear often blocks mercy. Here are three kinds of fear that can delay the process:

- *Fear of losing control or power.* To help your mate let go of her need to control the situation, demonstrate your trustworthiness and show that you understand the seriousness of what you've done. Let your spouse see that you have to live with the consequences every day; assure her regularly that you've learned a great deal about how deeply your actions have affected her. Show how you're taking steps to prevent the mistake from occurring again.

- *Fear of not being able to punish the wrongdoing.* Maybe your spouse is still in the anger stage and wants you to experience some of the hurt she felt. Be patient during this stage of the process, whether your mate is right or wrong. Pray for your spouse; ask God to reveal your broken heart and your desire to make things right. Eventually your spouse may start asking herself, *Why can't I forgive? What payoff am I getting out of not forgiving?* Questions like these often lead to healing, but it takes time.

- *Fear of forgetting what occurred.* Help your spouse realize that you don't expect her to not remember what happened. That's impossible. Explain that you simply look forward to the day when she will be affected less by your actions, and to the opportunity of proving your commitment to make your marriage healthy again. Be as understanding as possible. Impatience will only underline the suspicion that you don't care what your partner is struggling with.

3. *Seek outside guidance.* If necessary, ask a professional counselor or older Christian to help you and your spouse with the process. You might be surprised to know how many people you respect have struggled with and triumphed over issues of forgiveness. Make sure, though, that your spouse is open to this help. An outsider may be

perceived as a threat or as an additional source of embarrassment.

4. *Be honest with yourself.* It's easy to see your spouse's failure to forgive when you're confident that your heart is genuinely remorseful. But keep checking your own attitude and actions during your journey to forgiveness. Ask the following questions:

- *What exactly caused my spouse to be hurt?* It's easy to forget what the real issue is and focus on distractions.
- *What behaviors or attitudes do I hold on to that cause more hurt?*
- *What's my plan to make necessary changes?*
- *What might God be showing me in my spouse's inability to forgive?*

—*Mitch Temple*

## TAKING IT PERSONALLY

1. If your spouse were to write you a letter of forgiveness as James' wife did, what do you wish it would say?

2. What's one thing you can do this week to apply each of the following recommendations? (a) Demonstrate your trustworthiness; (b) show that you understand the seriousness of what you've done; (c) let your spouse see that you have to live with the consequences every day; (d) assure her regularly that you've learned a great deal about how deeply your actions have affected her; (e) show how you're taking steps to prevent the mistake from occurring again.

# How Can Faith Keep Us Together?

*27*

Every marriage needs a bond to sustain it during the trials that will surface. Is faith in Christ really the glue that can keep a marriage together?

After all, some statistics seem to indicate that evangelicals divorce at a higher rate than those with no connection to religion. As Glenn Stanton, director of social research and cultural affairs and senior analyst for marriage and sexuality at Focus on the Family writes, "We often hear that divorce rates among people who identified themselves with certain denominations and lived in the Southern Bible Belt states had higher divorce rates than people with no religious affiliation. . . . [But] religious commitment, rather than mere religious affiliation, contributes to greater levels of marital success."[1]

Stanton notes that sociologists David Popenoe and Scott Stanley explain that the "Bible Belt" statistics result mainly from higher poverty rates and marriage at younger ages—not religious participation. In fact, University of Virginia sociologist Brad Wilcox found that evangelicals who attend church regularly have a divorce rate 35 percent lower than secular couples, after adjusting for factors like economic and educational status.[2]

But how does faith make a difference?

When Kay and Carl married, they made a commitment to honor each other. They hoped nothing could break their bond. They had high moral values and a personal relationship with the Lord. Their security was in Jesus—not in themselves, not in each other.

They were beginning in the right direction. Could they stay the course?

It didn't take Kay long to realize that Carl had a lot of faults she'd failed to recognize. One was his inept handling of their money.

Kay had a choice. She could handle the problem in a way that was consistent with her faith, which took the authority of the Bible seriously. Or she could turn elsewhere for advice.

She decided to take an approach that echoed 1 Peter 3:3-6: "Your beauty . . . should be that of your inner self, the unfading beauty of a gentle and quiet spirit, which is of great worth in God's sight. For this is the way the holy women of the past who put their hope in God used to make themselves beautiful. They were submissive to their own husbands, like Sarah, who obeyed Abraham and called him her master. You are her daughters if you do what is right and do not give way to fear."

When Kay respectfully and graciously confronted Carl with their dilemma, he was able to hear her instead of being defensive. Now it was his turn to decide whether his response would reflect his faith.

He decided to apply principles he'd learned in 1 Timothy 3:3-6, especially the instructions to be gentle, not quarrelsome or proud or greedy. In particular, he didn't allow pride to get in the way of learning new budgeting methods.

In other words, faith helped keep them together.

Kay and Carl faced another challenge when it came to in-laws.

Carl's mother had never really been excited about her only son marrying anyone—including Kay. Every family gathering was uncomfortable for Kay, and she began to feel resentful. She wanted to yell at Carl and tell him to defend her.

Instead, she prayed about the problem. She asked God to make it clear to Carl what his role as a husband should be in this situation.

Before long, Carl was choosing to follow 1 Corinthians 16:13-14: "Be on your guard; stand firm in the faith; be men of courage; be strong. Do everything in love." He took a more active part in supporting his wife, and did it in a loving way. Once again, faith helped keep these spouses together.

Then came another challenge. Carl and Kay moved to another state, leaving the church that had been an awesome support system for them. Knowing what a difference faith had made to them individually and as a couple, they looked in their new location for the nurturing and fellowship of other believers. They found it in a church with solid teaching, where they began to volunteer. Again their faith provided resources that strengthened their relationship.

Faith helps keep couples together despite the smaller challenges of everyday life, too. When Carl offends Kay, for example, her understanding of what the Bible says about forgiveness is activated. So is her commitment to apply those principles. She knows that God has graciously extended forgiveness to her, and expects her to do the same for others (Matthew 18:23-35). This helps her to have a forgiving heart toward Carl, preventing a root of bitterness—a marriage killer—from taking hold. Forgiveness is a vital ingredient of the glue that holds marriages together.

So is fidelity. Carl and Kay have pledged to be faithful to one another, which might prove difficult for Carl in his job. He works with women who are congenial and attractive. All the temptations are there—travel, creative teamwork, the opportunity to share confidences. Carl isn't blind, but the eyes of his heart are enlightened (Ephesians 1:18). Having received the gift of a relationship with God, he's not about to mess it up. He chooses to "avoid every kind of evil" (1 Thessalonians 5:22). His commitment to Kay flows from his commitment to the Lord.

If you're a follower of Christ, staying together as a couple involves the same things that living your faith does—constantly putting aside pride, working daily on fully accepting God's forgiveness, and seeking to do what pleases Him. The following passage applies to marriage as it does to all of life: "Therefore, since we are surrounded by such a great cloud of witnesses, let us throw off everything that hinders and the sin that so easily entangles, and let us run with perseverance the race marked out for us" (Hebrews 12:1).

Can faith keep you together? God's Word says it can.

*—Betty Jordan*

## Taking It Personally

1. What role has faith played in your relationship with your bride (or bride-to-be) so far? If it hasn't played an important role, should you count on it to keep your marriage together?

2. Which of the following are you willing to do this month in order to build up your supply of "faith-based relationship glue"? (a) Join a small group Bible study; (b) pray regularly with your mate; (c) take turns reading from a book about spiritual growth; (d) work together in a church service project.

# What If an In-law Doesn't Accept Me?

## 28

Heather and Steve have been married almost four years. They love each other very much, but relationships with their in-laws have always been strained.

Heather feels Steve's mother is overly critical of how Heather parents the children. She also gets upset over her mother-in-law's statements about how Steve works much too hard; she sees them as attacks on her choice to be a stay-at-home mom.

Steve has great difficulty connecting with his father in-law, who seems to live for sports. When Steve and Heather visit his in-laws, Steve is especially disturbed to see Heather share her father's sports mania—leaving Steve feeling like an outsider.

It's normal to want to be accepted by your in-laws. But feeling that you *need* to be accepted can bring complications, causing you to be uncomfortable and unnatural around them.

Unrealistic hopes cause problems, too. Many parents are initially over-protective of their own child, or have expectations that no spouse can meet in the beginning.

Often new husbands and wives assume they'll be loved and accepted by in-laws on the merit of having married the in-laws' child. This may be the case, but it usually takes time to establish trust and respect. Just as it takes time to build other close relationships, gaining acceptance into a family doesn't happen instantly.

After all, you're stepping into a family with a long history of established bonds. Don't be too hard on yourself and expect too much. If your relationship with your own parents is wonderful, the one with your mother- and father-in-law may never measure up. If your relationship with your parents isn't good, you may be too needy and demanding in trying to make up for it.

The number-one factor in resolving problems of acceptance by in-laws is your spouse's support. As with all close relationships, it's an art to support your spouse without jumping into the fight or feeding his or her discontent.

Let's say that Heather and Steve have just returned from an extended visit with his parents. She declares: "I never want to stay with your parents again! Why doesn't your mother like me? She told me that she had you potty trained by age two and that you obeyed her without question."

In this case, Heather is being a little overdramatic and overly sensitive. How can Steve support her without reinforcing her exaggeration or condemning his mom?

He could say something like this: "Honey, I'm so sorry that you feel hurt by the things my mom says. But I know you're a terrific mother, and she'll come to see that, too. She also seems to remember me as much more perfect than I was. I can remember plenty of frustration and grief, but it's probably good that she doesn't remember all the tough times. I'll always support you in finding a time to share your feelings with my mom. I really think she likes you and can't help but love you as time goes on."

Or imagine that Ken has the complaint. "I don't want to spend more than one day at your parents' house ever again," he says. "I always feel like a third wheel. I know your dad hates the fact that I don't enjoy sports. You and he seem to be in your own little 'sports world.' What am I supposed to do, spend my time helping your mom in the kitchen?"

Heather might respond by reassuring Ken along these lines: "I'm so sorry that I haven't been more sensitive to your feelings of being left out during those times. You're right—sports has been the major thing Dad and I share. I know even Mom has felt a little left out when we obsess about it. Let's see if we can think of ways to connect when we're at my parents—all of us, including my mom. I know my dad primarily cares how I'm loved and taken care of, and there's no question about those things in my mind. Please give me a little sign if I forget it next time."

When it comes to dealing with an in-law who doesn't seem to accept you, here are the main principles to remember:

- Learn to support your spouse without getting hooked into taking sides.
- Encourage your spouse to share her feelings directly with you.
- Keep a sense of humor.
- Show your spouse that she is number one in your eyes.
- Don't take things too personally.
- Remember, building a relationship takes time.
- Forgive, forgive, forgive.
- Remember that you're loving your spouse by honoring her parents.

One more idea: When confronted with what feels like a no-win situation involving an in-law, use the "drop the rope" theory. Imagine a rope, the kind used in a tug-of-war. If you find yourself provoked, see that rope in your hands. You can choose to continue yanking on it—or drop it. Dropping it may sound as though you're giving in or giving up, but it's actually very empowering. It's also much more effective than tugging back and forth.

For Ken and Heather, a solution may look something like this:

- They discuss the things their in-laws say and do that tend to trigger anxiety and anger.
- They agree to act as "buffers" for each other against possible hard spots.
- They commit to forgiving any offense quickly.
- They plan to give the relationships time to develop.
- They start working as a team.
- They can even see some humor in learning to drop those "invisible ropes."

As a result, each of them feels more loved and supported. That helps them enjoy getting to know and appreciate each other's parents.

*—Romie Hurley*

## TAKING IT PERSONALLY

1. When was the last time that "dropping the rope" might have helped you get along with your in-laws? What did you do instead?

2. If your spouse (or spouse-to-be) could grant you three wishes concerning acceptance from your in-laws, what would they be? How could your mate make the situation less stressful for you (discuss your feelings, act as a buffer, work as a team, point out your good qualities to her parents, etc.)? Try requesting that help this week.

# How Can We Keep from Drifting Apart?

*29*

"We just drifted apart."

So many couples cite this as the reason for their divorce that you might think it's inevitable. Is it? If not, how can you prevent it?

Robin admits that she and her husband, Tony, are drifting apart. "We have different interests now. He's immersed in his work, and I'm at home all day with our three sons. I gave up my career to raise a family while Tony gets promotions. When Tony gets home, he has nothing left for me. He doesn't really love me."

Many couples seem to feel marriage is like selecting the right plane—and then putting it on autopilot. That's a good way to ensure that spouses eventually drift apart.

Here's how it often works: One partner is satisfied with the relationship as it is, but the other's needs are overlooked. In the case of Robin and Tony, Tony has been the mostly happy one. He has a beautiful wife, three great kids, a relationship with the Lord, and a job he enjoys. He's seen himself as having made the right choices— so from now on, it's smooth sailing. Autopilot has seemed to work for him.

Robin, on the other hand, is wondering whether she made the

right choice of "plane." She needs more of Tony's presence to feel valued.

In a bid for Tony's attention, Robin has started distancing herself from him. His reaction is to feel inadequate, disappointed in himself that he can't make his wife happy, unworthy of her love, and confused. He's thinking, *What am I doing wrong?*

Instead of disclosing her needs, Robin is expecting Tony to do some mindreading. When he fails, she withdraws her love. He, in turn, feels rejected and helpless to please her. Closeness evaporates, replaced by confusion and disappointment.

The result: Their relationship feels empty. They're drifting apart.

Robin and Tony need to understand that marriage is a growing, living relationship that needs nurturing. Before nurturing can be accepted, though, both partners have to be willing to take responsibility for their feelings and behaviors.

Using "straight talk" to acknowledge emotions without blaming can lead to resolving conflict. Robin could start the process by saying something like, "Tony, when I've had little adult conversation all day, I really need to talk with you."

Is this statement blaming? No. Is it clear what she needs? Yes. This will prevent defensiveness, contempt, and withdrawal.

Robin also can set the stage for solving the problem by putting the kids on a schedule that allows her "alone time" with Tony. The degree of closeness in a marriage reflects the overall climate in a home, and "climate control" takes spending time together.

Robin needs to know how to handle her resentment, too. When thoughts like *He doesn't really love me* arise, what should she do?

When such a thought strolls into the entryway of her mind, it doesn't belong to her yet; she doesn't have to feel guilty about it. But when she "camps on" this resentful thought instead of analyzing and rejecting it, it takes on a life of its own. She accepts ownership and buys into deception. She allows the thought to keep her from respectfully telling Tony what she's experiencing.

There's hope for Robin and Tony. They're both Christians who take their relationship with God seriously, and have been asking Him what to do about drifting apart. With His leading, they're working on making changes like these:

- becoming better listeners;
- taking responsibility for their actions and feelings;
- avoiding blaming;
- being more affectionate and considerate;
- becoming partners in parenting;
- respecting each other's differences;
- supporting each other in extended family conflicts;
- praying individually and as a couple;
- journaling their feelings individually to their heavenly Father;
- placing a priority on time together;
- submitting to God as their authority;
- being proactive by creating a plan.

There are as many reasons for drifting apart as there are marriages. But the way to prevent that drift begins with a single step: taking yourself off autopilot.

*—Betty Jordan*

## TAKING IT PERSONALLY

1. Are you more like Tony or
   Robin? Does taking your
   relationship off autopilot
   sound dangerous, freeing,
   pointless, tiring, or exciting?

2. If you find yourself thinking, *She doesn't
   love me* this week, what will you do? How
   will you avoid "camping on" that thought? How will you analyze
   and reject it? How will you respectfully tell your partner about
   your feelings?

# How Can We Keep
# the Romance Alive?

*30*

Romance has been described as "idealized love."

Does that mean it's only an infatuation between high school sweethearts? Is it a short-lived attachment? Is it even *meant* to last?

Megan says she and her husband, Terry, have lost the romance in their marriage. They have two children, and Megan spends every waking hour caring for the needs of her family. At the end of the day she's exhausted, with no energy for candlelight dinners.

What should Megan and Terry do? Is there a list of "rules for romance" they need to follow?

Not exactly. It's actually a deeper issue; the presence of romance reflects the overall quality of a maturing relationship.

A man who was one of four sons tells how, every night, his father would come home and walk right past his boys. He would go directly to his wife and give her a hug and a kiss. Then he would turn to the four little stairsteps who were watching, and say, "I think I am falling in love with your mom."

That man—and his sons—knew something about how romance can survive in a marriage.

So what can you do to help romance survive in yours?

1. *Recall your beginnings.* Remember when you first met and fell in love. What characterized your relationship? Did you listen to every word your intended said?

You probably were considerate and filled with respect. Each of you gave the other your complete, constant attention. You overlooked each other's faults and wanted to be together.

Was your love based on reality? Not the "reality" of annoying habits and thoughtless slights you may have catalogued since the honeymoon. But aren't the qualities that attracted you to each other just as real? Maybe it's time to rediscover them.

2. *Give up the spotlight.* Now that Megan and Terry have children, Megan can't give all her attention to Terry. Terry can't do that for Megan, either; he may be focusing on his work or a home project to make life better for his family.

Part of maturity is not needing to be the center of attention. Both Megan and Terry can demonstrate love for each other, but in new ways—indirectly as well as directly. As long as each of them views the other's role with respect and consideration, romance—idealized love—doesn't have to elude them.

3. *Live under God's authority.* Keeping romance alive is a lot easier when you're growing the fruit of the Spirit—love, joy, peace, patience, kindness, goodness (love in action), faithfulness, gentleness, and self-control (Galatians 5:22-23). When Megan and Terry submit to God, the spark of romance not only has a chance of being rekindled, but can become a radiant flame.

4. *Honor each other.* Romance certainly involves emotion. But it's also about valuing our spouses.

When Terry and Megan got married, they both felt love for one another. But when Megan was pregnant, she began to feel neglected by Terry, and a wound was opened. Terry sensed the distancing, and soon he felt unappreciated, too.

Gary and Norma Smalley offer this advice on honoring your spouse: "When you honor your wife, she will sense that nothing and no one in the world is more important to you. She won't have to wonder if she's number one—she'll know."[1] The same goes for a wife's treatment of her husband.

5. *Be honest.* Feeling guilty, Terry and Megan didn't tell each other about their resentment. This could be the beginning of a downward spiral if they don't start opening up. Resentment is an enemy of romance.

If you and your mate feel you can't be honest with each other, let a Christian counselor or pastor help get the conversation going.

Keeping romance alive requires effort and creativity. It means honoring one another by being honest, kind, and respectful in your responses, showing affection throughout the day without expecting sexual intimacy, having a regular date night, lighting candles or having a sweet fragrance in the bedroom, praying together, sharing feelings, and taking responsibility for your offenses. When these are standard operating procedure in Megan and Terry's home—or yours—romance won't be a thing of the past.

Romance is a living, growing love. Things that grow require "tending to." No one can do this alone. It takes both marriage partners giving their all; it takes reliance on the Holy Spirit to empower you, especially in the darkest hours.

God designed romance to be an ever-changing treasure. As your marriage progresses, will you allow the rosebud of romance to mature into full bloom?

—*Betty Jordan*

## Taking It Personally

1. What's the most romantic thing your bride (or bride-to-be) ever did for you? What's the most romantic thing you ever did for her?

2. What do you think romance could look like for the two of you five years from now? Fifteen? Fifty? As a couple, describe a "perfectly romantic evening" you'd like to have on your first wedding anniversary. Write down the description, save it in a "time capsule," and make plans to celebrate that anniversary in a way that reflects what you've written.

# SUGGESTED RESOURCES

*There are many helpful books and other resources to guide you through the early years of marriage. Check your local bookstore for the following:*

*Boundaries in Marriage* by Dr. Henry Cloud and Dr. John Townsend (Zondervan, 2002)

*The DNA of Relationships* by Gary Smalley (Tyndale House Publishers, 2004)

*For Women Only* by Shaunti Feldhahn (Multnomah, 2004)

*The Gift of Sex: A Guide to Sexual Fulfillment* by Clifford L. Penner and Joyce J. Penner (W Publishing Group, 2003)

*Great Expectations: An Interactive Guide to Your First Year of Marriage* by Toben and Joanne Heim (NavPress, 2000)

*Healing the Hurt in Your Marriage* by Dr. Gary and Barbara Rosberg (Focus on the Family/Tyndale House Publishers, 2004)

*Hedges: Loving Your Marriage Enough to Protect It* by Jerry B. Jenkins (Crossway Books, 2005)

*Hidden Keys of a Loving, Lasting Marriage* by Gary Smalley and Norma Smalley (Zondervan, 1993)

*His Needs, Her Needs: Building an Affair-Proof Marriage* by Willard F. Harley, Jr. (Monarch Books, 1994)

*How Do You Say, "I Love You"?* by Judson Swihart (InterVarsity Press, 1977)

*The Language of Love* by Gary Smalley and John Trent, Ph.D. (Focus on the Family/Tyndale House Publishing, 2006)

*Love and Respect* by Dr. Emerson Eggerichs (Integrity Publishers, 2004)

*Love for a Lifetime* by Dr. James Dobson (Multnomah, 2004)

*Love Must Be Tough: New Hope for Families in Crisis* by Dr. James Dobson (Multnomah, 2004)

*The Most Important Year in a Woman's Life/The Most Important Year in a Man's Life* by Robert Wolgemuth, Bobbie Wolgemuth, Mark DeVries, and Susan DeVries (Zondervan, 2003)

*Sacred Marriage* by Gary Thomas (Zondervan, 2002)

*Saving Your Marriage Before It Starts* by Les and Leslie Parrott (Zondervan, 1995)

*Surviving a Spiritual Mismatch in Marriage* by Lee and Leslie Strobel (Zondervan, 2002)

*Your Marriage Masterpiece* by Al Janssen (Focus on the Family/Tyndale House Publishing, 2008)

**The following booklets and recordings are available from Focus on the Family (call 1-800-A-FAMILY):**

*Accepting Your Mate's Differences* by Dr. Kevin Leman (Focus on the Family broadcast CD192)

*Building a Marriage That Lasts* by Dr. James Dobson (Focus on the Family booklet LF154)

*Learning to Communicate* by Gary Smalley and John Trent (Focus on the Family broadcast CD111)

*Nothing to Hide* by Joann Condie (Focus on the Family booklet F00038T)

# Notes

### Is It Okay Not to Have Kids?
1. Candice Z. Watters, "Defending 'The Cost of Delaying Marriage,'" *Boundless* webzine (http://www.boundless.org/2005/articles/a0001145.cfm).

### How Can Faith Keep Us Together?
1. Glenn Stanton, "The Role Faith Plays in Marriage and the Likelihood of Divorce," (Focus on Social Issues, July 8, 2005), found at http://family.org/cforum/fosi/marriage/divorce/a0037068.cfm.
2. W. Bradford Wilcox, "The Cultural Contradictions of Mainline Family Ideology and Practice," publication pending.

### How Can We Keep Romance Alive?
1. Gary and Norma Smalley, *It Takes Two to Tango* (Colorado Springs: Focus on the Family, 1997), p. 25.

# FOCUS <sup>ON</sup><sub>THE</sub> FAMILY®

*Welcome to the family!*

**W**hether you purchased this book, borrowed it, or received it as a gift, we're glad you're reading it. It's just one of the many helpful, encouraging, and biblically based resources produced by Focus on the Family for people in all stages of life.

Focus began in 1977 with the vision of one man, Dr. James Dobson, a licensed psychologist and author of numerous best-selling books on marriage, parenting, and family. Alarmed by the societal, political, and economic pressures that were threatening the existence of the American family, Dr. Dobson founded Focus on the Family with one employee and a once-a-week radio broadcast aired on 36 stations.

Now an international organization reaching millions of people daily, Focus on the Family is dedicated to preserving values and strengthening and encouraging families through the life-changing message of Jesus Christ.

## Focus on the Family Magazines

These faith-building, character-developing publications address the interests, issues, concerns, and challenges faced by every member of your family from preschool through the senior years.

| Focus on the Family **Citizen®** U.S. news issues | Focus on the Family **Clubhouse Jr.™** Ages 4 to 8 | Focus on the Family **Clubhouse™** Ages 8 to 12 | **Breakaway®** Teen guys | **Brio®** Teen girls 12 to 16 | **Brio & Beyond®** Teen girls 16 to 19 | **Plugged In®** Reviews movies, music, TV |

**FOR MORE INFORMATION**

**Online:**
Log on to www.family.org
In Canada, log on to www.focusonthefamily.ca

**Phone:**
Call toll free: (800) A-FAMILY (232-6459)
In Canada, call toll free: (800) 661-9800

# Make the most of your relationships with resources from Focus on the Family®!

From dating and engagement to the wedding and beyond, we're here to help your marriage thrive.

### First Comes Love, Then What?

Myths about finding Mr. or Mrs. Right are held to be true by too many men and women searching for that one-in-a-million match. It's time for a reality check. Filled with real-life examples and solid principles, this book will help both men and women learn to use their heads before losing their hearts.
Paperback F00727B

### Countdown for Couples

Research and common sense indicate that engaged couples will have stronger, more successful marriages if they participate in premarital counseling. Yet with all the planning that goes into a wedding, this important preparation can often be overlooked. *Countdown for Couples* delivers insight in an easy-to-use format and tackles important questions such as: *Are you ready for a lifelong commitment? What should you expect? And more!*
Paperback F00863B

### The Savvy Bride's Answer Guide

Your maid of honor might not tell you, but the price of your wedding dress isn't the only thing that may shock you about wedded bliss. During the first year of marriage, you're likely to face all kinds of surprises—from your in-laws' strange traditions to your groom's annoying tendencies. This friendly resource will smooth the road whether you've been engaged for 10 minutes or married for 10 months.
Paperback F00857B

### The Smart Groom's Answer Guide

Launching your lifetime love? Getting biblical answers is the smart thing to do! This book provides down-to-earth advice from a team of professional Focus on the Family counselors. You'll get the real story on questions like *What does it mean to be a husband? Why does she want to talk all the time? And more!* Ask now—or forever hold your peace!
Paperback F00856B

# marriage